WHY JOHNNY CAN'T
SING HYMNS

WHY JOHNNY CAN'T SING HYMNS

How Pop Culture Rewrote the Hymnal

T. DAVID GORDON

P&R PUBLISHING

P.O. BOX 817 • PHILLIPSBURG • NEW JERSEY 08865-0817

Printed in the United States of America

Library of Congress Cataloging-in-Publication Data

Gordon, T. David, 1954-
  Why Johnny can't sing hymns : how pop culture rewrote the hymnal / T. David Gordon.
      p. cm.
  Includes bibliographical references.
  ISBN 978-1-59638-195-7 (pbk.)
  1. Church music--Philosophy and aesthetics. 2. Popular culture--Influence. I. Title.
  ML3869.G67 2010
  781.87009'04--dc22

                              2010006410

This slender volume is dedicated to
the memory of our first child,

Marian Ruth.

Before leukemia took her at fourteen weeks of age,
she taught her parents the ancient Christian practice of
singing praise through tears.

Thou wast their Rock, their Fortress, and their Might;
Thou, Lord, their Captain in the well-fought fight;
Thou, in the darkness drear, their one true Light.
Alleluia! Alleluia!

O blest communion, fellowship divine!
We feebly struggle, they in glory shine;
All are one in Thee, for all are Thine.
Alleluia! Alleluia!

CONTENTS

122494

PREFACE

WHY WRITE ANOTHER BOOK about worship music? Hasn't enough already been said about this topic? And haven't most churches already considered the matter and made their choice? These are all understandable questions, and I myself often question whether any open minds still exist on the matter. But as I've read some of the very good material already written on the subject, I notice that some of the pertinent considerations have not been addressed. I teach an introduction to media ecology at Grove City College, and my studies in that field through the years have given me a different point of view. Media ecologists look at all media in a particular way. They view media both as social *constructs* (things that *reflect* cultural values) and as social *constructors* (things that *shape* cultural values). Media ecologists tend, therefore, to ask a range of questions that others do not. They tend, for example, to view pop culture itself as a medium, something created by a culture that, in turn, shapes the culture in particular ways. My small contribution to the discussion, therefore, resides in this media-ecological perspective. Most of the considerations I raise in this brief study, and the perspective from which I address those considerations, differ from most of what I have read on the topic, so I hope my voice will be a distinctive one in the chorus of voices addressing this matter.

Media ecologists are, effectively, a subbranch of cultural anthropologists. Cultural anthropologists have often observed the dialogical relationship between tools and their makers: we make tools, and tools make us. The tools we employ both *reflect* our priorities and values and reciprocally *shape* our priorities and values. If our culture invents the hoe, for instance, we can be sure that our culture is not a hunter-gatherer culture or a postindustrial culture, but an agricultural culture. Hunter-gatherer cultures do not need hoes—but if they were given hoes, they would eventually become agricultural cultures. The ability to till the soil and raise predictable crops would eventually terminate the nomadic lifestyle of the hunter-gatherer culture.

We make tools, and tools make us. This general outlook about toolmaking becomes more specific to media ecologists, who evaluate how the particular tools of human media both reflect our values and shape our values: how and why we make them, and how and why they make us. As a media ecologist in the tradition of the cultural anthropologists, I am willing to posit this thesis: we make song, and song makes us. I trust that the discussion will not be harmed by adding this point of view to it.

From this media-ecological perspective, a perspective I employed in my earlier *Why Johnny Can't Preach: The Media Have Shaped the Messengers*, I also note that an important question to raise is not merely whether we should sing contemporary songs versus traditional hymns.[1] An even more important

---

1. *Why Johnny Can't Preach: The Media Have Shaped the Messengers* (Phillipsburg, NJ: P&R Publishing, 2009), a media-ecological study of the influences of dominant cultural media on the sensibilities of preachers.

question is this: why is it that so many people effectively *cannot* sing traditional hymns? Why, for so many people, do these hymns seem foreign? Why do they seem so strange, unfamiliar, and inaccessible?

One of the larger themes of this book is that contemporaneity itself is a tacit or implied value, a value promoted by many factors in our culture, but few more so than the ubiquity of pop music. As "background" music, contemporary music is everywhere, and becoming even more widespread all the time. It permeates film, television, and commercials; we *hear* it on radio or CD or MP3 (though I doubt that anyone actually *listens* to it) while we brush our teeth, make our breakfast, and so on; we attempt (in my case, haplessly) to dine to it in restaurants; and with the popularity of the various personal listening devices, many individuals never unplug from it. Awash as our culture is in this type of music, it has seeped into our sensibilities in such a way that nothing that antedates it really *sounds* like music to us.

I notice, for instance, in "blended" or "supplemental" worship services that the congregation dutifully, and sometimes surprisingly heartily, sings the traditional hymns and musical rubrics, such as the *Doxology*, *Gloria Patri*, *Sanctus*, and *Agnus Dei*. But then when the guitars come out, and we sing the contemporary songs (with repeated refrains between the verses), the place takes on another aura: it gets funky. At this point, middle-aged women start to get down with Jesus, swaying and singing as they did thirty years ago at Grateful Dead concerts.[2] People

2. I am not unaware that in many cultures, music and dance are inseparable. In such cultures, all music is accompanied by some bodily motion. I am therefore not suggesting here that it is inappropriate for music to be accompanied by dance, or by dancelike

who would find it odd if we repeated the *Gloria Patri* or *Doxology* four times don't find it odd that we repeat the refrains to these choruses numerous times, even if they are less theologically significant. Why? Why this attitudinal shift, this plainly palpable difference in the way the traditional music is experienced and the way the contemporary music is experienced? Part of what I suggest as the answer is that my own generation began to embrace contemporaneity thirty to forty years ago, deliberately opposing ourselves to our parents and their traditions, introducing such value-laden adjectives as "hip" and "with it" to common vocabulary, effectively cutting ourselves off from previous human artistic expression—and none more so than *musical* artistic expression.

Thus, when such individuals began the child-rearing process, we baptized our children effectively into the name of the Hip, the With It, and the Contemporary. We pursued our "adult" lives, and nourished our children's lives, with a kind of benign contempt for any music that wasn't guitar-accompanied. When The Who's Pete Townshend sang "My Generation," he expressed the sentiments that shaped our generation, sentiments that have yet to be questioned by the subsequent generation, sentiments that perceive our generation as distinct from all that preceded it. At a subconscious level, then, saturated as we have been with contemporary-sounding music, we have reached the tipping point in our culture where any earlier music is foreign-sounding, whether much earlier music such as that

---

motions. To the contrary, I consider that to be a perfectly fair question of aesthetic theory to be settled on its own merits elsewhere. But I mention the matter here because it reveals that we *react* to contemporary-sounding music differently than we react to other types of music. As Ken Myers has observed, people often play "air guitar" while listening to rock; but almost no one plays "air violin" when listening to a violin concerto.

of Giovanni Pierluigi da Palestrina, Johann Sebastian Bach, or Franz Joseph Haydn, or even barely earlier music such as that of Tommy Dorsey, Glenn Miller, or Count Basie. The sixties is the watershed: everything before the sixties is "old"; everything after is "contemporary." More significantly, nothing before the sixties sounds much like music to us; it is as foreign-sounding to us as Oriental music is to most Western ears. What follows, then, is both an abbreviated exploration of why Johnny can't sing hymns and an even more abbreviated exploration of why I judge the situation to be unhealthy.

To illustrate the current situation, let us just step back imaginatively into my father's generation: those reared largely during the Great Depression. Commercial radio was not normally broadcast around the clock in most places during the twenties and thirties, and even where it was, not every family had a radio or, if they did, listened to it frequently. The radio was not playing in the background when my father's family purchased groceries or when they shopped for clothing. My father would have experienced music in four idioms, which were perhaps close to equally balanced. Every week of his life he heard sacred music at church on Sunday; around the house or while working, there would have been the occasional singing of folk music; on radio he would have occasionally heard an almost-equal blend of classical music and pop music (in his case, the pop music would have been that of Glenn Miller, Duke Ellington, Tommy Dorsey, and the like). Each of these four kinds of music, then, sounded equally like music to him. His sensibilities were shaped roughly equally by them, so each was accessible, each sounded familiar; more importantly, none sounded unfamiliar. Today, however, the average individual experiences no such balance. Some 95 percent or more of the music we hear today is pop. Only a small percentage of the population tunes in to classical radio stations; many churches no longer sing the historic hymns of the faith; folk music is almost unknown. We are surrounded by nearly ubiquitous pop music—so much so that nothing else really registers in our consciousness *as* music. If it is not accompanied by a guitar, if it is not accompanied by the predictable melodies and rhythms of pop culture, it just doesn't seem like music.

I do not approach the subject without prejudice. Somehow, I semi-survived being a child of the sixties and seventies. Along with my Led Zeppelin, Black Sabbath, ZZ Top (especially their earlier work), The Who, Traffic, Eric Clapton, and the Doors, I was and am able to listen to my late father's Duke Ellington or Benny Goodman with pleasure, and am also able to listen to Dietrich Buxtehude, Wolfgang Amadeus Mozart, and Johannes Brahms with pleasure.

Further, as a student (and teacher) of Greek for over thirty years, I observe that the noun *idiotes* (from the adjective *idios*, "one's own") was not originally a term of contempt (as our word *idiot* ordinarily is); rather, it was used to describe people who could speak only their own language, their own idiom, and not those of others. Paul used it this way when he instructed the Corinthians regarding praying in unknown languages: "Otherwise, if you give thanks with your spirit, how can anyone in the position of an outsider [*idiotes*] say 'Amen' to your thanksgiving when he does not know what you are saying?" (I Cor. 14:16; also v. 23). Though the Greeks did not intend the degree of insult that our English derivative ordinarily does, it did imply disapproval or regret that some individuals or cultures had cut themselves off from the greater empire and the greater project of humanity.

My own generation and my children's generation are—to use the Greek term—musical idiots. We think we are choosing to listen to pop music, when in fact we are *not* choosing, any more than a Kentucky coal miner flatters himself that he "chooses" English. He does not compare and prefer English to (for example) French; English is all he knows. So also, I fear that our generation, a generation that has so consciously cut itself off from the previous generations, thinks it is "choosing" to listen to contemporary music, when in fact, because of our earlier choices and the ubiquity of pop music in our culture, contemporary music is simply the only music that sounds, to our ears, like music. All previous music is as foreign to us as French is to the Kentucky coal miner.

What follows is intended to be *descriptive*. I am attempting to describe the current situation, and attempting to explain why nothing but pop music sounds like music to us. Those who dislike the book will object that it is not merely descriptive, but *prescriptive* and *proscriptive*. They will note that I am actually writing a critique of much contemporary worship music and a defense of the church's traditional music. There is some validity to this objection because, in order to make my point, I will at times indicate why I think contemporary worship music is often of a lesser literary, theological, or musical quality than most traditional hymnody. But I do this as a means to an end, not as an end in itself. My goal is to explain why we have a preference for music that is often literarily, theologically, or musically inferior, and I cannot do this by merely asserting that much contemporary worship music is inferior. So a portion of what follows is a candid discussion of the literary, musical, and theological criteria by which the church has ordinarily assessed worship music. And by those criteria, much (but not all) of contemporary worship music does not fare very well.[3] But again, what I say in this regard is merely a means to the end of a more important concern: to explain why, for the first time in church history, a generation finds itself so completely cut off from the traditional musical canon of the church.

I concede to my objectors, therefore, that there is indeed a prescriptive element to the book. But this prescriptive element (in which I attempt an abbreviated defense of the value of traditional worship forms, including traditional musical forms) is intended to serve the descriptive purpose of assessing why our generation finds the church's earlier musical traditions to be foreign, if not downright unpalatable. This, I submit, should not be deemed inappropriate, because description can have no purpose if it does not ultimately have some prescriptive or proscriptive consequences.[4] I am hoping that even those who

3. I will repeat the substance of this footnote toward the conclusion of the book also, lest it be missed. Some contemporary worship music would satisfy the criteria of earlier hymnbooks. Stuart Townend has written contemporary hymn lyrics that satisfy such criteria. His "In Christ Alone" and "How Deep the Father's Love" would, in my judgment, satisfy many of those criteria, and ought to be seriously considered for inclusion in subsequent hymnals. Further, as the matter has progressed in the last decade, I believe it would be useful to distinguish "contemporary hymns" from "contemporary praise choruses" because there are idiomatic and musical differences between them. They are both "contemporary," however, and for the purposes of this volume I will focus on that particular distinctive.

4. Students of media ecology will recall that this was precisely the difference between Marshall McLuhan and his student Neil Postman. In most of McLuhan's writings, he professed only to be describing the new electronic- and image-based environment, without prescription or proscription. But his student Neil Postman consistently took a different point of view, and argued that the

employ contemporary worship music exclusively will therefore find the book helpful or insightful, even if they may disagree with my occasional value judgments. Indeed, I have submitted the manuscript to a number of friends who have substantial sympathies with contemporary worship music for their feedback, and most of them, while not in entire agreement with my value judgments, have found it helpful to read the manuscript.

As a final introductory thought, this book is, in some senses, a companion to my earlier *Why Johnny Can't Preach: The Media Have Shaped the Messengers.* There, I attempted to observe some of those cultural changes that have had the effect of impoverishing the pulpit. Here, I attempt to observe the cultural changes that, in my judgment, have impoverished congregational praise. If, as most orthodox thinkers have said, worship is a dialogue between God and his people, and if, as I argue, both his primary means of addressing us (preaching) has declined and our primary means of addressing him (praise) has declined, then worship itself has declined profoundly and almost totally. That the combined force of these two modest monographs might stimulate some reconsiderations of such decline (and its potential reversal) is the author's prayer.

Questions for Reflection

I. Is it true that "we make tools, and tools make us"? Can you think of examples of how the use of certain tools or instruments shapes their users?

---

ultimate goal of all description was evaluation. As he often put it, all description takes place, and ought to take place, within some moral or ethical (or in this case aesthetic) context.

2. How is it significant that the Greek adjective *idiotes* means "one's own"? What parallel can be drawn between church worship today and a concern in the New Testament?
3. Is the primary thrust of the book descriptive, or is it prescriptive/proscriptive? Why?

ACKNOWLEDGMENTS

ALL OF US WHO WRITE are aware of our limitations. But when writing on a topic such as this, one is especially aware of those limitations. To write about this area requires, ideally, that one be conversant with culture analysis and media ecology; that one be trained in the theological disciplines, and especially in worship, liturgy, and hymnody; and that one be trained musically. Few of us have technical training in all these areas; I surely do not. I have a lifelong nonprofessional interest in culture analysis (which may have been triggered by my initial reading of Tocqueville, and by many years as a colleague of David F. Wells, one of evangelicalism's most astute observers of American culture); I teach an introduction to media ecology. I have three graduate degrees in biblical and theological studies, pastored for nine years, and taught a course on Presbyterian government and worship at Gordon-Conwell Theological Seminary for many years. But although I can read music, I do not currently play a musical instrument, have never played piano (a serious liability if one is to understand the properties of music), and have not formally studied music history or theory. I have therefore benefited greatly from other churchmen and musicians who have been kind enough to read drafts of this book.

Pastorally, there are few men whose wisdom I appreciate more than Irfon Hughes, Charlie Wingard, and Greg Reynolds, each of whom has been kind enough to read the draft and offer numerous helpful suggestions. Additionally, the rector of our church, Ethan Magness, has not only read and commented on the manuscript, but also contributed to many insightful conversations about liturgy, worship, and worship music. Musically, some of my more boneheaded errors have been gently corrected by Grove City colleagues Dr. Joshua Drake and Dr. Paul Munson, and by Tenth Presbyterian's Dr. Paul S. Jones, each of whom has managed to find something encouraging to say despite my numerous sophomoric observations and blunders. Theological and ecclesiological insight (and encouragement) has been generously offered by Michael Horton. Jeff Schooley read the manuscript painstakingly, making many detailed observations that have improved it substantially. Marvin Padgett and his colleagues at P&R Publishing were delightful to work with on the previous volume, and have been the same on this project.

Of course, I assume entire responsibility for the defects of the final manuscript, and wish to absolve the above-mentioned readers from association with those defects. Yet those defects would have been far more numerous and glaring apart from their patient work, which is here very sincerely acknowledged.

INTRODUCTION: MY PASTORAL CONCERNS

DURING MY NINE YEARS as a full-time pastor, one of my weightiest responsibilities was that of preparing the weekly worship service. Though I had studied worship (and, to a lesser degree, liturgy) for well over a decade, and had even taught Presbyterian worship at Gordon-Conwell Theological Seminary, this study and teaching had aided me only in addressing some of the larger and broader questions. Our service in New Hampshire, for instance, followed substantially John Calvin's Strasbourg Liturgy. But among the weightiest matters I faced each week, even within an already-settled overall theory and structure, were the choices regarding *particular* forms of worship.

We had a corporate prayer of confession, for instance, but which one would I choose for each week of the year, and why? What made the decision difficult was my awareness that, on any given Sunday, the choice to use one particular prayer of confession was also a choice to exclude other options.[1] The same was true for the hymns I selected. Even in

---

1. By the time I left, we had a group of thirteen prayers of confession and employed them, in order, four times annually—providing, I hope, some variety and some continuity.

retrospect, I believe I can honestly say that I never selected a hymn that was heterodox or unlawful. Yet I was quite aware, every single week for nine years, that to select four hymns on a given Sunday was to reject (at least for that Sunday) probably a thousand other Christian hymns in the English language. This is what made the matter so weighty. While the elders of my church gave conscientious and diligent oversight to the overall issues of worship, ordinarily I was the one who chose which, of the known English hymns, to exclude from my congregation's experience.

To make the responsibility more manageable on a weekly basis, I began with a review of the particular hymnal that our congregation employed. Over a number of months, I studied the 700-plus hymns in our hymnal, excluding some for theological reasons and some for musical reasons, and ended up with a provisional list of about 150 that I was confident were appropriate to corporate Christian worship, about 500 that I was confident were not appropriate (many for musical reasons), and another 50 that would need further study. This helped, but I still faced the weighty duty every week of determining which of the 146 would be sacrificed to the four. That is, it wasn't the choice of what to *include* that made the matter weighty; it was the choice of what to *exclude*. I, and largely I alone, would decide which hymns would instruct and inform the Christian consciousness and sensibilities of my congregation and, more importantly, which would not. If I excluded the wonderful hymns of Paul Gerhardt, most of my congregation would never know them. If I excluded William Cowper's hymns, most of my flock would never hear them. If I withheld from them Bernard of

Clairvaux's 1153 "O Sacred Head, Now Wounded," most would worship and live and face their persistent mortality without it.[2]

I was not and am not a student of music, musicology, or hymnody. I had been reared in the church, however, and knew that my own religious experience and consciousness was profoundly shaped by the music of the church. At an existential level, I knew that what I sang to God was as significant in forming religious consciousness as what he said to me (and us) through Scripture and preaching. I knew personally the power of singing thanks and praise, and I knew the sustaining power of good, well-known hymns.

Several years before I began my pastorate, my wife and I had learned that our first (and, at the time, only) daughter, Marian Ruth, had leukemia. We moved to Boston Children's Hospital, where we lived with her for the remaining eight weeks of her life. We took a Bible with us, and a hymnal. Ordinarily, when my wife showered in the morning, I held Marian in the crook of one arm, and the hymnal in the other, and sang to her. Fortunately for me, she was not a music critic, and she always seemed comforted by her dad's voice in song. And the hymns surely helped her father, who knew what she did not—that she had virtually no chance of surviving.

2. Set to Hans Hassler's 1601 musical setting, translated into German by Paul Gerhardt in 1656 and into English by James Waddell Alexander in 1830, and, yes, harmonized by an obscure German composer named Johann Sebastian Bach in 1729. From Bernard to Alexander, 677 years passed. It took nearly seven centuries for this hymn to travel from medieval Latin to modern English. After seven centuries of input from some of the church's finest musicians and theologians (James W. Alexander was the son of Princeton Seminary's first professor, Archibald Alexander), who was I to prevent my church from knowing it?

One morning, with Marian in my arm, I began singing the well-known Evensong by Henry F. Lyte, "Abide with Me." The hymn is almost perfectly paired to its stately, trusting musical setting by William H. Monk, and I had been familiar with it since a young man. I could almost sing it from memory, and was proceeding well until its concluding stanza, which I sang as much *for* her as *to* her:

> Hold thou thy cross before my closing eyes;
> Shine through the gloom, and point me to the skies:
> Heav'n's morning breaks, and earth's vain shadows flee:
> In life, in death, O Lord, abide with me.

This was a bit too much for a heartbroken new father, and it took me three efforts to get through it. Little Marian smiled patiently. She didn't live long enough to feel the weight of guilt, sin, shame, or even, I suspect, mortality. She therefore also didn't live long enough to know the sustaining power of God's grace, how rich it is to be surrounded by the prayers of friends and family, or the comforting, courage-begetting gift of a well-written hymn. Her father, fool though he was and is in many other ways, knew all of these rich realities.

Because of my experience with Marian, which was merely a microcosm of my entire experience to that point, I knew that the hymns that accompany one's life are one of life's richest treasures. And so when I became responsible for selecting hymns for my congregation on a weekly basis, I knew that I was equipping them to live either well or not so well. The hymns to which I introduced them, and those that I withheld from them, would be a significant component of their religious experience.

Therefore, one of the more mystifying aspects of the conversation about contemporary worship music is the glibness with which it is often discussed. Frequently, almost invariably, people say things such as, "Well, it's not really that important," or "It's really just a matter of taste." It is difficult for me to think of any other important dimension of Christian worship and liturgy that would be dismissed so blithely:

"It's just the Lord's Supper, after all; take a chill pill."

"Hey, it's only a prayer."

I have difficulty imagining my Baptist friends saying, for instance, "Well, they're only baptizing babies; it's no big deal."

Yet this is the situation we find ourselves in. While some have called the discussion of contemporary worship music the *worship wars*, because the introduction of contemporary worship music has been divisive in some particular congregations, few people actually consider the arguments for the alternatives. That is, most Lutherans know something of the history of the theological discussions that have led to Lutheran distinctives, and could speak about them. Most Baptists know something of the rationale for why they reject paedobaptism. But we rarely find a similar awareness of the rationale for including or excluding contemporary worship music. There appears to be a resistance to taking the matter seriously, as a significant liturgical innovation. Unlike the Reformers, for instance, who argued that the Roman liturgy had serious errors in it, proponents of contemporary worship music do not wish to charge its opponents with error; they merely wish to say that they prefer to do things differently.

This resistance to taking the matter seriously is itself a by-product of a particular culture's unstated values: pop culture and pop music, largely created by and for commercial purposes, resist serious analysis. Commerce wishes us to give attention to its commercial messages, but commerce never argues its case for *why* we should give attention to its messages. Similarly, commerce surrounds its messages with programming (as a means of enticing our attention to its messages) and does not argue the case for why (or whether) we should give attention to that programming either. Commerce desires that both its commercial messages and the programming around it be consumed without critical thought. Commerce, then, has an enormous interest in our not taking such questions seriously or self-consciously.

But the question of the role of music in individual or cultural life is very serious. Some universities and colleges offer courses on the sociology of music, and extremely important works have been written on the subject, by such influential thinkers as Max Weber.[3] To dismiss the cultural effects of music as insignificant, or merely a matter of taste, is like dismissing the study of sociology itself as merely a matter of taste. Yet neither is merely a matter of taste; each is a significant field of intellectual study. Even at a nonacademic or nonphilosophical level, we observe that music is socially and sociologically significant: we sing about what is important to us. Nations compose national anthems; each branch of the American armed services has its own song; lovers compose love songs; and European soccer fans boisterously sing the songs of their respective teams throughout soccer matches.

3. Don Martindale, Johannes Riedel, and Gertrude Neuwirth, trans. and ed., *The Rational and Social Foundations of Music* (Carbondale, IL: Southern Illinois University Press, 1958). Also cf. Augustus Delafield Zanzig, *Music in American Life, Present & Future* (London: Oxford University Press, 1932); Alphons Silbermann, *The Sociology of Music*, trans. Corbet Stewart (London: Routledge & Kegan Paul, 1963); and Wayne D. Bowman, *Philosophical Perspectives on Music* (Oxford: Oxford University Press, 1998).

Music may be religious or profane, sublime or mundane, pious or pernicious, but music is *not* insignificant. It would not be a universal reality in all cultures if it were insignificant.[4]

And surely no question related to the behavior within God's house is insignificant, almost by definition. For one thing, it is, after all, *his* house, and all that we do in it ought to be done with a due grasp of the significance of there being a dwelling-place on earth where God can be met at all. The Christian assembly is sometimes referred to as the *house* or *household of God*, in passages such as these:

> I hope to come to you soon, but I am writing these things to you so that, if I delay, you may know how one ought to behave in the household of God, which is the church of the living God, a pillar and buttress of truth. (I Tim. 3:14–15)

> For it is time for judgment to begin at the household of God; and if it begins with us, what will be the outcome for those who do not obey the gospel of God? (I Peter 4:17)

Assembled believers are similarly referred to as God's *temple*: "Do you not know that you are God's temple and that God's Spirit dwells in you? If anyone destroys God's temple, God will destroy him. For God's temple is holy, and you are that temple"

---

4. I am not suggesting that it is sinful or shameful for an individual to be unfamiliar with the sociology or philosophy of music. Each of us is ignorant of many things. I, for instance, do not understand the fundamental theorem of calculus, and could not explain differentials or limits (when "x approaches zero," my understanding of the fundamental theorem approaches zero also). But I do not deny that the theorem exists, nor do I deny that it is important. Similarly, it is fine for some individuals to take no interest in the sociology of music, or in musicology per se; but it is not fine for them to deny that such areas of study exist, or to deny that significant individuals have taken the matter seriously.

(I Cor. 3:16–17; cf. also 2 Cor. 6:16; Eph. 2:21). These New Testament passages reflect a fairly serious biblical teaching about the house of God.

In the Old Testament Scriptures, the building of a house for God, whether temporary (tabernacle) or permanent (temple), was very serious business. Doubters are invited to read the precise instructions about the details of the construction of the tabernacle in Exodus 25–27, 35, 36, and 38–40. They are similarly invited to consider that one of the Old Testament covenants itself was the covenant for the lineage of David to build a permanent house of God, and they are reminded that David himself was not permitted to build this house because of God's judgment against him. Perhaps Jacob was the first to grasp this profundity after his dream about the reuniting of heaven and earth. Jacob's response was this:

> "Surely the LORD is in this place, and I did not know it." And he was afraid and said, "How awesome is this place! This is none other than the *house of God*, and this is the gate of heaven." (Gen. 28:16–17, italics mine)

House of God, biblically, is redemptive, and communicates nothing less than the reversal of the curse-banishment of Genesis 3, and the restoration of a once-banished race to the presence of its Maker. Therefore, it is not too much of a stretch, biblically, to say that the house of God is a very significant matter, and that when the New Testament assembly is now referred to by the name *house of God*, it is a rich and significant reality. For this assembly to be designated by God as his *house* is itself a redemptive truth of uncanny importance, indicating that the dwelling-place of God is again with humans. For this reason, then, no discussion about what takes place in the house of God is insignificant. Some discussions may be less significant than others (the color of the carpet in the church sanctuary is less significant than, for instance, the frequency of Communion), but every aspect of the house of God is significant, including how it worships God in song.

Another reason that no question regarding the house of God can be insignificant is that worship song itself is an extremely significant matter in the Holy Scriptures. One entire book of the canon (the Psalms) is exclusively a collection of such songs. One suboffice within the order of Levitical priests was that of singer or chorister (e.g., 1 Chron. 6:33; 9:33; 15:16–19; 2 Chron. 5:11–13). Moses wrote Psalm 90, and sang both the song of the sea (Ex. 15) and the song of the ark of the covenant (Num. 10:35–36) with his fellow Israelites. Deborah and Barak celebrated Yahweh's military deliverance in song (Judg. 5). Zechariah and Mary, respectively, anticipated the births of John (Luke 1:68–79) and Jesus (Luke 1:46–55) with song. Many biblical passages expressly command God's people to "sing to the LORD" (Ex. 15:21; 1 Chron. 16:23; Pss. 95:1; 96:1–2; 98:1; 147:7; 149:1; Isa. 42:10; Jer. 20:13; cf. also Ps. 100:2; Isa. 49:13; Eph. 5:19; Col. 3:16). The apostle Paul wrote instructions about singing in the Christian assemblies (1 Cor. 14:15); and perhaps most importantly, John's visions of the redeemed saints in heaven routinely portray them as engaged in worship song:

And they sang a new song, saying,

"Worthy are you to take the scroll
    and to open its seals,

29

for you were slain, and by your blood you ransomed people
     for God
   from every tribe and language and people and nation."
     (Rev. 5:9)

And they were singing a new song before the throne and before
the four living creatures and before the elders. No one could
learn that song except the 144,000 who had been redeemed
from the earth. (Rev. 14:3)

And they sing the song of Moses, the servant of God, and
the song of the Lamb, saying,

"Great and amazing are your deeds,
   O Lord God the Almighty!
Just and true are your ways,
   O King of the nations!" (Rev. 15:3)

These passages in Revelation reflect the earlier, prophetic antici-
pation of redemption as characterized by singing:

The whole earth is at rest and quiet;
   they break forth into singing. (Isa. 14:7)

And the ransomed of the LORD shall return
   and come to Zion with singing;
everlasting joy shall be upon their heads;
   they shall obtain gladness and joy,
   and sorrow and sighing shall flee away. (Isa. 35:10)

Sing, O heavens, for the LORD has done it;
   shout, O depths of the earth;

break forth into singing, O mountains,
  O forest, and every tree in it!
For the LORD has redeemed Jacob,
  and will be glorified in Israel. (Isa. 44:23)

And the ransomed of the LORD shall return
  and come to Zion with singing;
everlasting joy shall be upon their heads;
  they shall obtain gladness and joy,
  and sorrow and sighing shall flee away. (Isa. 51:11)

Break forth together into singing,
  you waste places of Jerusalem,
for the LORD has comforted his people;
  he has redeemed Jerusalem. (Isa. 52:9)

For you shall go out in joy
  and be led forth in peace;
the mountains and the hills before you
  shall break forth into singing,
  and all the trees of the field shall clap their hands.
    (Isa. 55:12)

Biblically, then, neither music nor song is merely a matter of entertainment or amusement. Both are very serious business, both culturally and religiously. Song is the divinely *instituted*, divinely *commanded*, and divinely *regulated* means of responding to God's great works of creation, preservation, and deliverance. Worship song is both the remarkable privilege and the solemn duty of the redeemed. Therefore, to suggest that worship song is "merely" or "just" anything, whatever that "anything" is, is to deny the very teaching of Scripture about the importance of worship song in God's economy—an importance so great that it characterizes the life of the redeemed in the world to come. Thus, the unfortunately common statements, by both proponents and opponents of contemporary worship music, that this is "merely" a matter of taste or preference are erroneous and must be regarded as unbiblical.[5]

This unbiblical posture, that worship song is merely a matter of amusement or entertainment, and therefore merely a matter of personal preference or taste, does not arise because people desire to resist the teaching of the Holy Scriptures. Rather, it arises from a culture that has come to be characterized, as Neil Postman argued, by amusement.[6] In such a culture, in which we are surrounded by amusement, and in which music is perhaps the primary *form* of amusement, it is not surprising that even Bible-believing people have unwittingly adopted such an anti-biblical stance. They simply aren't aware of the conflict between the teaching of the Bible and the values of our culture on this point. Their error, therefore, is an understandable error, and should not be regarded as deliberate or high-handed rebellion. On the other hand, I must candidly state that I judge it to *be* an error.

Imagine, for instance, what it would be like to live in a world whose only music were to be found on Saturday at the local Jewish synagogue, where the cantor chanted prayers or

5. With regard to contemporary worship music, one rarely encounters the comment "merely a matter of taste" in print; but in practice, it is one of the most common things people say.

6. *Amusing Ourselves to Death: Public Discourse in the Age of Television* (New York: Viking, 1985).

Scripture in the refined intonation that results from his special training. If this were the only exposure we had to music, we would instinctively regard *all* music as sacred music. We would regard it virtually as a sacrament: a special religious ordinance instituted by God as a means of communing with him. Or imagine a world in which the only music were what we call *sacred music*, such as the hymns of Luther and Cowper, the cantatas of Bach, the oratorios of Handel, or the wonderful *Requiem* by Johannes Brahms—no Frank Sinatra, no Cole Porter, no Eric Clapton, Jimi Hendrix, or ZZ Top, and—perhaps mercifully—no Madonna, Pink, or 50 Cent. Again, in such a world, music *itself* would be construed as a distinctly religious reality, a rare thing encountered only when we encountered the sacred. Well, this imaginative world *is* the biblical world. Song is distinctly religious in the Bible; all music, biblically, is religious music.

But our culture is the mirror opposite of this biblical world. Music is nearly ubiquitous. We shop to it, work to it, play to it; our movies and television have musical sound-tracks; we cannot find a quiet restaurant to dine in because "background" music is always present. And our hapless young people are all 'podded up, shuffling around wherever they are with buds in their ears. (I've even encountered them when I've been backpacking, 'podded up while tramping along the trail, oblivious to what was once termed *musica mundi*, deafened to it by some pop artist's recording.) Music, by its very ubiquity in our culture, necessarily becomes mundane rather than sacred. And once our sensibilities regard music as mundane, it inevitably becomes "merely" music, and therefore not a thing to be rigorously studied. Theological seminaries might very well teach rigorous academic courses on the sacraments, for instance, expecting students to be conversant with the positions and arguments of various views of the sacraments, but they do not teach similarly rigorous courses on music. Music, for our culture, is "just music."

As I suggested above, *worship song* is in a different category from *music*, and should be so treated. To illustrate, suppose we compared *public speaking* to *preaching*, and asked whether they were the same thing. Well, they certainly are similar things. Each is public, and each consists of a discourse being given; so they share some common traits. But one is divinely instituted as an aspect of the meeting of Christians, and the other is not. One is said to be chosen by God: "it pleased God by the foolishness of preaching to save them that believe" (I Cor. 1:21 KJV). One can construct a biblical doctrine of preaching; one cannot as easily construct a biblical doctrine of public speaking. In some of Paul's letters, he corrects the manner or content of preaching. Thus, preaching is divinely instituted for particular purposes, and is regulated by the Scriptures in accord with those purposes.

Similarly, worship song may share many traits with what we generally call *music*. But it is a particular thing. It, like preaching, is divinely commanded, and the Scriptures record this divine institution. Worship song, like preaching, is regulated by apostolic authority, and corrected when it needs to be corrected. Like preaching, inspired examples of worship song are recorded in the Scriptures. So while worship song shares some common traits with what we call *music*, it has distinctive traits as well; and we offer it to God as an act of obedience to his revealed will. Therefore, every consideration regarding it should be undertaken in a manner that reflects Christian obedience.

To treat the house of God or its activities as insignificant, or unworthy of serious Christian reflection, or to treat worship song as though it were nothing more than a matter of amusement or entertainment to be governed by personal preference, is to disregard or disagree with the teachings of the Holy Scriptures regarding both.

Over twenty-five years ago, I was discussing some aspect of church life with a fellow student at Union Theological Seminary, Milton Winter.[7] Both of us were working our way through our respective PhD programs, and both of us were active, interested churchmen. Milton proposed a challenge to me: "David, you write the systematic theologies, I'll write the hymnals, and we'll see who influences the church more." I was not so foolish as to take Milton's challenge. I understood, as he certainly did, that few things influence our Christian life more than how we sing praise to God. Both he and I are somewhat slack-jawed at the glibness with which people now speak about singing God's praise, as though it were an inconsequential matter. As the editors of the old *Trinity Hymnal* said in the preface, "It is well known that the character of its song, almost equal with the character of its preaching, controls the theology of a church."[8]

7. Dr. R. Milton Winter is now the pastor of the First Presbyterian Church in Holly Springs, Mississippi. What he articulated in his brief challenge was the old thesis *Lex orandi, lex credendi*: "The law of prayer is the law of belief"; how we worship shapes how we believe.

8. *Trinity Hymnal* (Philadelphia: Great Commission Publications, 1961), vi.

What follows is an extremely abbreviated list of the considerations that have caused me to be wary of using contemporary Christian music in worship services at all, to object to its common use, and to zealously oppose its exclusive use (*common* meaning using it regularly, perhaps equally with earlier forms of worship music, and *exclusive* meaning using it to the exclusion of such earlier forms). I don't intend to conduct a full discussion of each of the considerations, but I hope in each case at least to demonstrate that the consideration is worthy of our attention. And in each case, I attempt, albeit briefly, to indicate why I believe the consideration militates against the widespread use of contemporary worship music.

Questions for Reflection

1. Which is the weightier responsibility the author faced when he was a pastor: which hymns to *include* in a service of worship, or which hymns to *exclude*? Why?
2. Does music play a significant role in individual or cultural life, or an insignificant role? Why?
3. What is the theological significance of "God's house"?
4. Do the Holy Scriptures address worship song rarely or frequently? Do they grant worship song a significant or insignificant role in the life of the believing assembly?
5. Biblically, is music a matter of entertainment? How do you know?
6. Biblically, is worship song a duty? What is a verse that supports your answer?

7. In our contemporary American culture, is music primarily a matter of entertainment? If so, how does that influence our discussion of worship song or worship music?

8. Is it true and/or significant that "every consideration we undertake regarding it [worship song] should be done in a manner that reflects this to be an act of Christian obedience"?

I

INTRODUCTORY
CONSIDERATIONS

WORSHIP ITSELF is one of the most difficult things for Christians to discuss because their attachment to it is, understandably, emotional. As the primary means by which we meet with God in this life, public worship is very significant to us. It is very difficult for us to consider "giving up" public worship *as we have known and experienced it*, in exchange for some yet-unknown form. Music is also one of the most difficult things for Christians to discuss dispassionately, for similar reasons. Like worship, music is a reality that involves us emotionally and sometimes deeply, and therefore it is difficult for us to establish the philosophical distance necessary to evaluate it on aesthetic or musical grounds.

Worship music, then, is almost hopelessly impossible to discuss because it combines the passion we feel about worship with the passion we feel about music, and the whole enterprise becomes so fraught with emotion that philosophical distance is extremely difficult for most to acquire. Nonetheless, it is our duty, once we raise the subject, to do the best we can to evaluate it with all the resources available to us.

Further, it is also our duty to employ charity in discussing "polemical" theology, or controversial theology.[1] That is, the duty to love our neighbors does not cease here, and it is contrary to the law of Christ to dismiss the arguments of another by attacking the person's motives. On both sides of this question, I have often witnessed a descent into an attack on the motives of others: "Contemporaneists (or traditionalists) are just selfish; they just want things their way." According to the Westminster Larger Catechism (no. 145), among the sins prohibited in the ninth commandment is "misconstructing intentions, words, and actions." Unless we are certain that we understand the intentions of another, we run a grave risk of misconstructing them, which is a violation of the law of charity. None of us wishes our own intentions to be misconstrued, and therefore we are not at liberty to misconstrue the intentions of others.

Further, and logically, all such arguments *ad hominem* are irrelevant. They are irrelevant, as all *ad hominem* arguments are, because if a malicious person proposes a truth, it is not for that reason less true. If Adolf Hitler, for instance, believed in gravity, this would not mean that gravity does not exist. Such arguments are also useless because not one of us can claim to have perfectly pure motives; therefore, if we were to exclude from the discussion those whose motives are mixed, no one could enter this (or any other) discussion.

1. Those interested will want to consult the timeless counsel in the essay by a former colleague at Gordon-Conwell Seminary, Dr. Roger Nicole, entitled "Polemic Theology: How to Deal with Those Who Differ from Us," available at http://www.founders.org/journal/fj33/article3.html.

40

Some readers will have difficulty following portions of the discussion because they know so little about pre-contemporary Christian hymnody. My students, for instance, occasionally refer to "traditional" hymns, and when I ask them to mention one, they often choose one that is, in fact, quite new, almost contemporary. In a "mixed" musical service, for instance, they once selected "How Great Thou Art" as the traditional hymn—supposing, I guess, that the *thou* suggested an Elizabethan origin. But the hymn is quite new, written in Sweden in 1885 (by Carl Gustav Boberg), and not translated into English until 1953 (by Stuart Hine). In English, it is only one year older than I am. We live in a remarkable moment indeed when a hymn that is merely a century old, and in our own language only a half-century old, is regarded as traditional. Most of the Christian tradition never heard or sang this hymn. Indeed, most even of the English Christian tradition never heard this hymn; yet it is regarded as traditional. The point is significant, however, because I will suggest that *traditional* and *contemporary*, in the present discussion, have nothing to do with dates, history, or chronology. The terms are employed idiomatically, to refer to Christian hymns that have different musical properties.

Further, and the reason I mention the matter here, we face the challenging circumstance that many voices in the discussion know nothing of Christian hymnody prior to the nineteenth or twentieth century (which is precisely the moment when some of us think it began a downward spiral). They often equate *traditional* with organ-accompanied hymns, for instance, even though organs were uncommon in the Protestant tradition (both because of expense and because of musical and theological considerations) until the mid- to late nineteenth century. Thus, a young person reared in anything like a typical evangelical church knows only two things: nineteenth-century, sentimentalist revivalist hymns, and contemporary praise choruses; and they think the argument *against* the latter is an argument *for* the former. My students routinely assume that I am defending Bill Gaither or Fanny Crosby when I express reluctance about praise choruses. Yet those who know me well know that I carry no brief at all for Fanny Crosby or Bill Gaither, and those who were members of the church I pastored for nine years will testify that neither Bill nor Fanny made any appearances in my bulletins.

Why This Question Now?

For nineteen centuries, all previous generations of the church (Greek Orthodox, Catholic, Protestant, or Revivalist), in every culture, employed prayers and hymns that preceded them,[2] and encouraged their best artists to consider adding to the canon of good liturgical forms. That is, none were traditional, in the sense of discouraging the writing of new forms; and none were contemporary, in the sense of excluding the use of older forms. So why now this insistence that many, most, or all forms of worship be contemporary? My father's generation did not demand that all hymns be written in a big-band idiom, and mine did not demand that they be written to sound like Eric Clapton or The Who. So why do

2. John Calvin's Strasbourg Liturgy, for instance, was entitled *A Form of Prayers according to the Pattern of the Ancient Church*. And while we have since discovered ancient prayers that Calvin's generation was not aware of, the title is a clear indicator of Calvin's *attempt*.

we now find something unique in the history of the church: a considerable number of people who appear to believe sincerely that it is not merely permissible, but in some senses necessary or preferable to jettison hymns that previous generations employed? Why?

I ask the question partly rhetorically, but also because I honestly think that one cannot address the matter well without first wrestling with this. The issue is not whether it is permissible for a given generation to continue to encourage gifted artists to create forms of worship that may assist the church in her worship; this has never, ever been denied, and is not now denied by anyone.[3] The question is: Why do so many people appear to find it impossible or unprofitable to use the earlier forms? Why this craving for what sounds contemporary? Why can't Johnny sing hymns? Many people appear hesitant to answer this question, and some even evade it by reasoning that, for whatever reason, people today find contemporary musical forms attractive and noncontemporary musical forms unattractive, and that therefore we *must* provide such forms to them. But why should the sensibilities of those who may not even know God, or the sensibilities of a commercially driven, banal culture, rule in the worship of God? To employ a self-conscious argument *ad absurdum*, suppose we reached a point thirty years from now where the prevailing popular musical idiom of our culture were gangsta rap: would we then be required to worship exclusively in this idiom? Would this musical idiom be adequate or appropriate to the task?

---

3. Even exclusive psalmists, for instance, do not object to the composing of new musical settings of metrical psalms.

Up to twenty years ago, the members of hymnal-revision committees ordinarily had a group of six to ten musical, liturgical, literary, and theological criteria that helped them determine which hymns ought to be retained in, deleted from, or added to a new hymnal.[4] In contrast, many circles today have effectively only *one* criterion for choosing worship music: it must sound contemporary.[5] So now a criterion never before employed by anyone anywhere has become effectively the *only* criterion employed. And this has happened (as far as I know) without any study committees by any denominations.

That is, in my judgment, the essence of the question boils down to a cultural value, as invisible as radon gas, that has been unwittingly embraced by the church: *contemporaneity.* Contempo-

---

4. The preface to the *Trinity Hymnal*, for instance, mentions the goal of compiling a hymnal that has three traits: "truly ecumenical . . . , theocentric in orientation, biblical in content" ([Philadelphia: Great Commission Publications, 1961], v). Its successor volume (1990) reaffirms this threefold goal, and also mentions the desire that the hymns selected be "faithfully based on God's Word, clearly teach the doctrines of grace, and facilitate the biblical worship of God among his people" (Preface, *Trinity Hymnal* [Suwanee, GA: Great Commission Publications, 1990], 8).

5. Charles Wesley was surely one of the most prolific, and arguably one of the more accomplished, hymn-writers in the English-speaking world. According to William J. Reynolds and Milburn Price, in their *A Survey of Christian Hymnody*, 4th ed. (Carol Stream, IL: Hope Publishing, 1999), 60, Charles Wesley wrote at least 6,500 hymns. Yet not all his hymns succeeded in making their way into the hymnal. *The United Methodist Hymnal* (Nashville: United Methodist Publishing House, 1989) has 862 hymns, only 41 of which were written by Charles Wesley. So of the 6,500 hymns that Wesley wrote, only 41 are found in the hymnal of the denomination most influenced by him. Only one hymn out of every 158 he wrote made its way into the hymnal. In percentage points, that is barely over one-half of 1 percent. Are our contemporary hymn-writers superior to Wesley? Probably not. Is their success rate higher than one in every 158 they write? Of course it is, because unlike Wesley, they get a "free pass." As long as their music sounds contemporary, virtually every other criterion for measuring hymns is discarded.

raneity is more an aesthetic value than an ethical value; but it is a value, a sensibility, that considers the past passé. No other generation ever before found itself so utterly distant from the art forms (or other cultural expressions) of previous generations. Yet this generation finds itself there. And the so-called worship wars are, in my estimation, like the radon detectors in our basements: they alert us to something in our environment that we would otherwise not notice. Most of what follows are the considerations that I believe, at a minimum, need to be addressed before we can determine whether contemporaneity, like radon, is both invisible and harmful or whether, like oxygen, it is invisible and harmless.

The so-called worship wars in the churches reflect the so-called canon wars in the universities in the 1980s. In those wars also, there was a revolt against the so-called Western canon—a canon judged to be "irrelevant" (or worse) to us. The same language is employed in the worship wars. Ironically, nearly all conservative Christians took one side in that discussion, and find themselves on the other side in the present one. Why did we defend the West's *literary* canon (the product, largely, of non-believers), but repudiate its *hymnody* canon (the product, largely, of believers)? Why did we trace our literary and philosophical roots to the past, but not our musical roots to the past? Why did we warn our culture not to cut itself adrift from its intellectual and literary roots, but not warn our church not to cut itself adrift from its liturgical, aesthetic, and hymnic roots?

One of the most common misunderstandings that make this matter difficult is that the pro-contemporary people almost always consider their concerns (that worship be conducted in forms that are *contemporaneous*) to be analogous to Martin

Luther's concern that worship be performed in the *vernacular*. Luther wanted worship to be conducted in a known language (following Paul) because worship that is unintelligible cannot be edifying. As Paul said:

> For if I pray in a tongue, my spirit prays but my mind is unfruitful. What am I to do? I will pray with my spirit, but I will pray with my mind also; I will sing praise with my spirit, but I will sing with my mind also. (I Cor. 14:14–15)

Luther therefore translated prayers and hymns from Latin into German. But there is no evidence at all that Luther ever said that worship had to be conducted in contemporary-sounding musical idioms. To the contrary, what evidence exists suggests that Luther believed in what we now call *sacred music*—music that is deliberately and self-consciously different from other forms of music. He and others of his generation often wrote new musical tunes, for the distinctive purpose of accompanying hymns. And at any rate, *vernacular* and *contemporary* mean different things, and therefore an argument for one is no argument for the other. Luther did not argue that a prayer or hymn had to sound *contemporary*; he argued that it had to be *intelligible*, and therefore conducted in the vernacular language of a given culture. It is simply historically false to recruit Luther into this discussion. Yet the fact that he manifestly did consult earlier liturgies and translate portions of them into German is evidence that he exhibited no concern for that which was contemporary, and a very self-conscious concern to conserve and preserve forms from the past. His concern was for intelligibility, not contemporaneity.[6]

What I am looking for is an argument that actually addresses the crux of the decision that many churches have now made: that the criterion of contemporaneity trumps all the criteria of all the hymnal-revision committees that ever labored. I put it that way because, with very few exceptions, the contemporary praise choruses that are actually selected would not ordinarily satisfy the criteria that previous hymns had to meet to get into the hymnals. These included, but were not limited to, items such as the following:

- theologically orthodox lyrics
- theologically significant lyrics
- literarily apt and thoughtful lyrics
- lyrics and music appropriate to a meeting between God and his visible people
- well-written music with regard to melody, harmony, rhythm, and form
- musical setting appropriate to the lyrical content

By these criteria, only the most artistically gifted (or arrogant) of generations could possibly imagine that it could, in a single generation, be expected to produce a body of hymns that surpassed all previous hymns and rendered them obsolete.

6. Paul Jones has conclusively demonstrated that Luther never employed "bar songs" as melodies for his hymns, though he did employ what is called "bar form," an A-A-B structure, as a musical device, which may have contributed to the present misunderstanding of the matter. Cf. the chapter "Luther and Bar Song: The Truth, Please!" in his *Singing and Making Music: Issues in Church Music Today* (Phillipsburg, NJ: P&R Publishing, 2006), 171–78.

So the question remains: Why does *contemporaneity* deserve to be included as a criterion at all, much less as a criterion more important than all of these? Why are there not signs outside churches that read: "Theologically Significant Worship," or "Worship Appropriate to a Meeting between God and His Assembled People," or "Worship That Is Literarily Apt and Thoughtful"? Why do the signs say "Contemporary Worship," as though that criterion were itself worthy of promoting?

The True Comparison Is to the Psalms

Proponents of contemporary worship music ordinarily compare it to what they call *traditional hymns*, and argue that some of the best of the one are nearly as good (or as good) as the worst of the other. Fair enough, but is that our standard? Study the biblical psalms and ask whether, on lyrical grounds, the various forms of contemporary worship music demonstrate anything like the theological or literary integrity or profundity of the individual psalms. The best hymn-writers have made this their goal and standard; indeed, Isaac Watts took the very substance of the 150 canonical psalms and wrote Christological, metrical paraphrases of them.

Lawful Is Not Enough

Paul, addressing the matter of food offered to idols in I Corinthians 10:23, said, "All things are lawful," but not all things are helpful. "All things are lawful," but not all things build up. There is some debate whether his "All things are lawful" is merely hyperbole, indicating that many *more* things are lawful in the Christian covenant than in the Mosaic, or whether it is

Paul's rhetorical concession to the libertines at Corinth, who wrongly taught that all things *are* lawful. In either case, Paul's point is that even when we have determined that a thing is lawful, we have not finished our evaluation. Other considerations must also be brought to bear, such as whether it is helpful and whether it edifies.

This deeper look is important to our circumstances because some people wish to terminate the discussion at the level of what is lawful. If older musical forms are lawful, and if newer musical forms are lawful, then the whole question is *merely* a matter of taste, and nothing else can be said. This un-Pauline way of viewing the matter, I might add, is particularly tempting to those who favor the use of contemporary-music forms, since virtually no one has ever suggested that older forms, such as the *Gloria Patri* and *Doxology*, are unlawful. But followers of Paul (and therefore followers of Holy Scripture) cannot stop with the question of what is merely lawful. Whenever we choose one thing over another, there must be some reason, some rationale, for determining, at least in that particular circumstance, that the one thing is in some ways, for some purposes, superior to the other. Each of these various ways of making the decision is an issue of judgment that takes place *beyond* the mere consideration of what is lawful.[7]

---

7. John M. Frame's insightful book on this topic may suffer a bit from this tendency. It seems throughout that much of Professor Frame's argument is for the lawfulness of contemporary worship music, or at least an argument that contemporary worship music is not unlawful. His point is entirely well taken, but the point is not enough. The question is whether as a genre contemporary worship music is superior to hymnody as a genre—or, as I will put it, whether it is sufficiently superior to replace all the criteria by which previous hymnody was evaluated. Cf. his *Contemporary Worship Music: A Biblical Defense* (Phillipsburg, NJ: P&R Publishing, 1997).

To illustrate, suppose we asked whether it is lawful to accompany the singing of God's praise with a kazoo. Well, the Holy Scriptures do not contain a list of approved and disapproved musical instruments, so we really could not say, on explicit scriptural grounds, that kazoo accompaniment is unlawful. Would that settle the question? Would any churches adopt the kazoo as their accompanying instrument on the mere ground that it is not unlawful to do so? I think we know what the answer is. None would select the kazoo. But in not selecting the kazoo, they are suggesting, rightly in my judgment, that other considerations come into play: aesthetic questions, media-ecological questions, musical questions, form and content questions, cultural-value questions, and so on.

Similarly, my friends in the free-church movement[8] commonly and rightly remind me that they are "free" to employ spontaneous prayers—prayers that have not been composed or approved earlier by some ecclesiastical group. I agree with them; it is lawful to offer extempore prayer in worship. But the fact that it is lawful to do so does not mean that any *given* extempore prayer is as good as or better than *another* extempore prayer, and it does not mean that a given extempore prayer is better than some common prayer, previously composed. That it is lawful to consider choosing x does not mean that x is a better choice than y.

---

8. I realize that most refer to the phenomenon as the *free-church tradition*, but I refer to it as the *free-church movement*, on two grounds. First, it self-consciously distinguishes itself from any ecclesiastical tradition (and therefore, out of fairness, we should not misconstrue it as a tradition). Second, it is not a tradition in any ordinary sense, identifiable by some creedal or liturgical heritage (and therefore should not be dignified by the term *tradition*).

What follows, then, is a collection of those extralegal considerations that I judge to have bearing on the question. In each case, I state the matter briefly. Those who wish to think well about the matter will need to unpack each of those considerations substantially.

Questions for Reflection

1. Why is it difficult to discuss either worship or music dispassionately?
2. What was the title of Calvin's Strasbourg Liturgy, and why is the title significant?
3. What is *contemporaneity*?
4. The so-called worship wars in the church reflect what other earlier wars in our culture? What was the basis of those conflicts, and what is a key difference between the two?
5. Is there any historical evidence that Martin Luther desired hymns to be contemporary-sounding? Does evidence exist to the contrary? How is this significant?

2

AESTHETIC RELATIVISM

AESTHETIC RELATIVISM was a commonplace in the twentieth century, and will probably remain so in the twenty-first.
Aesthetic relativism states that there are no standards by which
artistic creativity may be measured; it is merely a matter of taste.
But such relativism may be as unbiblical as (or, as I think, *more*
unbiblical than) ethical relativism. In the first twenty-five verses
of the Bible, God is presented as a Creator; and the human,
whose creation is recorded in verse 26, is said to be the "image"
and "likeness" of God. While this image may include more than
creativity, it certainly cannot exclude creativity. The only thing
expressly affirmed about God prior to Genesis 1:26 is that he
creates. So when the text then says (four times) that the human
is made in God's "likeness" or "image," there is the strongest
implication that the human is essentially (not incidentally) a
creator.[1] And God's creative activity in the Genesis narrative is
not merely practical (what we would call the creativity of the

---

1. G. K. Chesterton's classic, *The Everlasting Man* (New York: Dodd, Mead & Co.,
1925), eloquently makes the point (among others) that humans are not *incidentally*
creative, but *essentially* creative, creative in the very center of our being.

artisan); his creative activity is also beautiful (what we would call the creativity of the artist). The garden that God made for Adam and Eve to cultivate was "pleasant to the sight and good for food" (Gen. 2:9); it was both lovely and life-sustaining, both beautiful and practical.

Ultimately, then, God himself is our aesthetic standard, just as he is our ethical standard.[2] As bearers of God's image, we have as our creaturely duty to imitate him in all the ways a creature can imitate the Creator, and surely this means that we are, like God, to make things that are beautiful or practical. Whenever we make something, we imitate God; and the evaluative question then becomes: have we made something well, as God makes things well?

Thus, when I cook dinner at our house, the meal I prepare should provide nourishment and should be pleasant to eat; it should be both pleasant and practical. I say it *should* be because it is not merely a matter of taste (the Gordons enjoy good food); it is a matter of imitating God well or imitating God less well. Now, the standards by which we evaluate creativity may be difficult to develop, and those standards might be more difficult to develop in some fields than others (perhaps it is easier to evaluate literature than architecture, for instance). That the task of establishing aesthetic criteria may be difficult, however, does

2. It may be that some aspects of God's creative activity have not been disclosed to us. But some things have been disclosed to us, and those things must be considered. God, for instance, not only makes, but observes and evaluates what he makes. In Genesis 1, he observed six times that what he had made was "good," and on the sixth day he observed all that he had made and judged that it was "very good." The garden into which he placed the first humans was "pleasant to the sight and good for food," both of which are expressions of judgment or evaluation. To surrender or abdicate the responsibility to observe and evaluate our creations is to abdicate this aspect of the *imago Dei*.

not mean that we should abandon the task. After all, the task of establishing ethical criteria is also difficult, and we have not abandoned that task. Christians routinely produce books, essays, and articles (not to mention sermons) about ethical matters, even though such matters are sometimes difficult. It should be the same way with matters of aesthetics.

Even non-Christian or nonreligious thinkers recognize the profound importance of aesthetics. Aristotle (4th century B.C.) wrote a significant treatise on it, and Longinus (c. 1st century) wrote about it; each of these was aware that others had articulated significant and serious opinions about aesthetics before them. It is not surprising, then, that students of the classical era have said things such as this: "The truth of art is higher than the truth of fact."[3] And as regards musical aesthetics, musical historians remind us of riots that occurred in the nineteenth and twentieth centuries when significantly innovative classical music was first performed by composers such as Hector Berlioz, Richard Strauss, Igor Stravinsky, Erik Satie, and Béla Bartók. To suggest that musical aesthetics is an insignificant matter, then, requires either dismissing or disagreeing profoundly with the entire Western tradition prior to the mid-twentieth century, Christian or otherwise.

In the current situation, one of the most frequently repeated errors regarding our evaluation of contemporary worship music is that it is "merely" a matter of taste. Such dismissive comments should be resisted. When arguments are made (on any

3. W. Hamilton Fyfe, Introduction to Aristotle's *Poetics*, Loeb Classical Library vol. 23 (Cambridge, MA: Harvard University Press, 1927), xvii. Students of literature will recall similar sentiments from Sir Philip Sidney's sixteenth-century *A Defence of Poesie*, in which he argued that fiction (*poesie*) was a more suitable arena for communicating truth than history or philosophy.

side of the discussion), they should be seriously entertained, weighed, and rebutted, not merely dismissed on the erroneous ground that human creativity is "merely" a matter of taste. Human creativity is a matter of imitating God the Creator; it may very well be the *most* significant thing humans do, so it is not "merely" anything, and it is surely not "merely a matter of taste." Indeed, in the current situation, for some individuals the *only* aesthetic criterion they recognize is contemporaneity. Think of it: A church has a sign that reads "Contemporary Worship," as though sounding contemporary were the only criterion that mattered. All the criteria by which previous hymns were evaluated are tossed aside, and this new criterion replaces them all (or moves to the top of the list of criteria). But why? Why does this criterion trump the other criteria? Some of the things God makes are new, such as a newborn child; but other things God has made are old, such as the Grand Canyon, the earth itself, and the universe. So in God's case, his creativity is not measured by the time in which the creativity took place; it must satisfy other criteria.

Indeed, when people talk about "contemporary" music, they are not, in fact, referring to the date of composition. The people who promote contemporary music, for instance, are not promoting the hymns of a twentieth-century hymn-writer such as E. Margaret Clarkson (b. 1915; d. 2008), whose hymns, though recently written, do not *sound* as though they were recently written. Nor are they promoting the fourteen hymns cowritten by the late James Montgomery Boice (d. 2000) and Paul S. Jones, written just a little over a decade ago.[4] Thus, not

4. *Hymns for a Modern Reformation* (Philadelphia: Tenth Presbyterian Church, 2000).

only is *contemporary* not an adequate or appropriate aesthetic criterion, it is not even an *accurate* criterion. People who use it actually mean something like this: a cluster of musical choices (primarily that the song be accompanied by a guitar) that have the aggregate effect of making a piece of music *sound* as though it were recently composed. What we call *contemporary music*, then, is actually music that sounds contemporary. Using such language would clarify the conversation, but it still would not answer the question of why some people prefer music that sounds contemporary. And it still would not justify *contemporary-sounding* as an aesthetic or liturgical criterion, at least without further argumentation.

Questions for Reflection

1. What is the premise of aesthetic relativism?
2. What is the relationship between the image of God and creativity?
3. According to the Genesis narrative, is God's creativity merely practical? If not, what other quality is reflected in God's creativity? Support your answer from the Genesis narrative.
4. Is aesthetic relativism an old idea or a comparatively new one? Cite some examples.

3

FORM AND CONTENT

MEDIA ECOLOGISTS, aesthetic theorists, and some linguists discuss the relationship between content and form, between a message and the vehicle that carries the message. The late Librarian of Congress Daniel J. Boorstin put it well:

> When Michelangelo in the traditional story explained that he carved his statue of David simply by taking away the superfluous marble, he meant that his peculiar vision dwelt somehow in that particular block of stone. Sculptors always, of course, choose a piece of marble because it is well suited to the figure they have in mind; and they often shape the figure to the marble's flaws. *Every artist marries form to matter:* he sees his poem in words, his painting in oils on canvas, his statue in stone, his building in some specific material.[1]

Adjusting this idea to worship music, there is a relationship between the message of the lyrics and the musical setting of those lyrics. The lyrics may very well constitute "the content" in

---

1. *The Image: A Guide to Pseudo-Events in America* (New York: Atheneum, 1975), 118, emphasis mine.

some senses, but the musical choices are part of "the content" also; otherwise, why not simply speak the words as a prayer? As we have already seen, proponents of contemporary worship music sometimes appear to be dismissive when the issues of musical form are raised, as though such issues were "merely" matters of musical taste. They may be matters of taste, yes, but they are not "merely" matters of taste. We would consider it in poor taste for someone to show up at a funeral in a clown suit, or to attend a wedding wearing a mask of Edvard Munch's *The Scream*. Not every tune is a good vehicle for every set of lyrics; some are more fit than others. And in theory, some musical choices could virtually never be an appropriate form for singing God's praise (such as accompanying them on a kazoo).

So the fair question is how the *form* of contemporary pop music shapes the *content* of what is placed in it. If the form, for instance, is deliberately contemporary-sounding, does this suggest that the lyrical message is also fading, transient, or ephemeral? Would it make good sense, for instance, to take the lyrics of something like "O God, Our Help in Ages Past" and put it into a contemporary-sounding musical form? I suspect not; the form would then make the content a different thing, and create a kind of dissonance. A hymn such as this, whose lyrics expressly call attention to God's providence in the past, cannot sound contemporary without there being a disconnect between the lyrics and the musical score.

Indeed, since contemporary pop music has been developed for commercial reasons, and is almost exclusively associated with fairly superficial amusement, one must raise the question whether a musical form so associated with such superficial amusement is ever an appropriate vehicle for a religion that requires repentance, sacrifice, obedience, and selflessness. No one has ever written a requiem, for instance, to be accompanied by three people playing guitars. Why? Because death is still (for some of us, anyway) a fairly serious matter, and guitar-playing just doesn't sound serious; it sounds like casual amusement.[2] I notice that when my students get married, they almost always have some classical music or traditional hymns in their wedding, even if every other week of the year they attend a church that uses contemporary music in its worship. What's going on here? Well, the students apparently (and rightly, in my opinion) judge that a wedding is a significant and serious occasion, so they accompany it with, yes, significant and serious music. But worship, I believe, is also significant and serious, and so how can we accompany worship with forms that are judged to be neither significant nor serious? I believe the marriage between Christ and his bride, the church, is more significant than any merely human marriage. And if our meetings on the first day of the week remember and celebrate the relation of Christ to his church, then we should employ forms that are as significant and serious as the content.

Some culture observers, notably Ken Myers, David Denby, Martha Bayles, John H. McWhorter, and Todd Gitlin, observe that pop culture is essentially trivial.[3] Television, pop music,

2. Classical guitar is a notable exception to this general observation, but probably not one in a hundred people in our culture has ever heard a piece of classical guitar music.

3. Ken Myers, *All God's Children and Blue Suede Shoes* (Westchester, IL: Crossway Books, 1989); Martha Bayles, *Hole in Our Soul: The Loss of Beauty and Meaning in American Popular Music* (Chicago: University of Chicago Press, 1996); John H. McWhorter, *Doing Our Own Thing: The Degradation of Language and Music and Why We Should, Like, Care* (New York: Gotham, 2003). David Denby primarily reviews films for the *New Yorker*, but also wrote the fine media-ecological treatise *Great Books* (New York: Touchstone,

and the other vehicles of pop culture are essentially trivial, ironic, or both. Denby, writing about his young son Max, put it this way:

> Even if the child's character is not formed by a single TV show, movie, video or computer game, the endless electronic assault obviously leaves its marks all over him. . . . The child survives, but along the way he becomes a kind of cynic; or rather he becomes an ironist, a knowing ironist of waste. He knows that everything in the media is transient, *disposable*. Everything on television is just for the moment—it's just *television*—and the kids pick up this derisive tone, the sense that nothing is truly serious.[4]

And Todd Gitlin said this:

> To put this another way: alongside specific effects, much of the time the everyday noise of media is the buzz of the inconsequential, the *just there*. This is neither the media's downside nor their saving grace. The buzz of the inconsequential is the media's essence. This pointlessness is precisely what we are, by and large, not free *not* to choose.[5]

Perhaps not everyone would agree with every aspect of their analyses, but if even a substantial minority of the culture associates contemporary music with the trivial, the inconsequential, or

---

1996). Todd Gitlin is a culture critic, most widely known for his book on the 1960s, *The Sixties: Years of Hope, Days of Rage* (New York: Bantam, 1993), but who more recently wrote *Media Unlimited: How the Torrent of Images and Sounds Overwhelms Our Lives* (New York: Henry Holt, 2002).

4. Denby, *Great Books*, 71.

5. Gitlin, *Media Unlimited*, 9.

the ironic, why would the church wish to use a form associated with the trivial or ironic, and employ it for worship? Is the content of worship trivial or ironic?[6] And if not, then why attempt to put serious content into a nonserious form? People may be amused by it, and some may tap their feet to it, but would Jesus have addressed the rich young man in such a tone?

Questions for Reflection

1. Is it true that form shapes content? Give some examples.
2. Some cultural observers suggest that pop culture is ordinarily trivial, banal, or ironic. Are they right? What makes you say so?

6. I don't suggest that irony is sinful or inappropriate to all settings. The fourth Gospel abounds in irony, for instance, as Paul Duke has ably demonstrated (Paul D. Duke, *Irony in the Fourth Gospel* [Atlanta: Scholars Press, 1985]). And surely there is profound irony in the idol-polemic in the Old Testament, as the psalmist observes that the idol-makers craft idols whose eyes do not see and ears do not hear, and "those who make them become like them" (Ps. 115:8). Professor Greg Beale of Wheaton College (soon to take a post at Westminster Seminary in Philadelphia), a former colleague of mine at Gordon-Conwell, was the first to point out to me how often biblical judgment is ironic.

4

META-MESSAGES

GERARD I. NIERENBERG wrote *Meta-Talk: The Guide to Hidden Meanings in Conversation* in 1973 to discuss what we now call *meta-messages*: nonverbal messages that go along with our actual words. Our body language, our tone, or other behaviors sometimes communicate a different thing from our words. Nierenberg noted that the nonverbal messages sometimes carry a different, or even conflicting, message from our verbal message. A student might tell me, for instance, that he "really likes" one of my classes, but I notice that he cuts class about a third of the time (or surfs the Internet behind his laptop screen during class, a practice that I judge to be ruder than simply cutting the class—but I digress). He says with his words that he likes the class, but his actions send a different message. Some of these meta-messages are probably conscious, and others might not be, but we never wish to send conflicting messages.

Meta-messages may attend the various things that we do liturgically in worship. Theoretically, the same inconsistencies that occur between our meta-messages and our other messages might occur when we worship. We might *say*, for instance, that we take God and faith seriously, but *do* things that seem contrary to that message. We might *say* that our worship is God-centered, but *do* things that belie this statement. We might *preach* that the way is narrow that leads to eternal life, but then *do* things that suggest otherwise. We might *say* that we wish to resist conformity to the world, but then *act* as though the world's ethos were our own.

Specifically, there are two areas in which contemporary worship music may send a meta-message that is contrary to the interests and values of the Christian faith. The first of these is contemporaneity itself, and I have some thoughts to share about that topic below. But another is triviality or banality. Many students of pop culture have suggested that artistically, pop culture is neither beautiful nor ugly; it is banal, trivial, or inconsequential. Ken Myers has especially made this point, but the point has also been made by people such as Todd Gitlin and John McWhorter.[1]

Commercial interests joined forces with mass media (originally radio, but later television also) to create pop music; it did not exist before. Pop music is a form of music designed to appeal, in some way, to the masses. If there were no mass media, pop music would not and could not really exist. Once it exists, however, it serves commercial purposes. Businesses purchase airtime to advertise their products, and they want to sell many products. Therefore, the fee structure for commercial advertisement is based on the size of the

---

1. Todd Gitlin, *Media Unlimited: How the Torrent of Images and Sounds Overwhelms Our Lives* (New York: Henry Holt, 2002); John H. McWhorter, *Doing Our Own Thing: The Degradation of Language and Music and Why We Should, Like, Care* (New York: Gotham, 2003).

audience; stations with large audiences can command higher prices than those with small audiences. But no one tunes in to a radio or television station for the commercials; we tune in for the programming.

So there's this very basic tension in all commercial broadcasting. The broadcasters and their advertisers are interested in the *commercials*; the audience is interested in the *programming*. As long as both parties are content to put up with the interests of the others, everyone is happy. But because the advertisers want a large audience, the producers of the programs must make them easily accessible to the population at large. They cannot produce programming that is profoundly offensive, and they cannot produce programming that is difficult to follow, programming that requires a steep learning curve. So what do they produce? Programming that is fairly insignificant. In the case of music, they produce music that does not require concentrated effort to appreciate, preferring instead music that is fairly simple and straightforward. In short, they produce music that is fairly insignificant, trivial, or banal. It cannot, ordinarily, last an hour (as a symphony with four movements might), and it cannot be musically demanding. For commercial reasons, therefore, pop culture and pop music cannot be either beautiful or ugly;[2] pop music must be easy,

2. Though Martha Bayles notes that in our situation, pop music has been permitted to be ugly and offensive in some ways, a subculture of rebellion and unrestraint has now come to be, if not the main culture itself, a significant part of that culture, to which commercial interests are willing to appeal. *Hole in Our Soul: The Loss of Beauty and Meaning in American Popular Music* (Chicago: University of Chicago Press, 1996). Her point is well taken, but not fatal to the thesis here. Attending a rock concert where the performers make obscene gestures is different from tuning in to commercial radio or television. There, commercial forces must be assured of a large audience. If the culture becomes crude enough, then and only then can we

and therefore it must be fairly inconsequential. Demanding pieces of music, such as the string quartets of Béla Bartók, would be commercial disasters.

But now, is worship inconsequential, trivial, or insignificant? Is meeting with God a casual, inconsequential activity, or a significant one? Is religious faith itself insignificant? If the music or lyrics of our hymns are insignificant or inconsequential, do they not send the wrong meta-message? Does not their very commonness, their mundaneness, their everydayness, their inconsequentiality suggest precisely the wrong thing? The lyrics of a hymn might say, "Holy, holy, holy," but the music might say, "Ho-hum, ho-hum, ho-hum." In such a case, the meta-message competes with and contradicts the message. Neil Postman rightly said: "I believe I am not mistaken in saying that Christianity is a demanding and serious religion. When it is delivered as easy and amusing, it is another kind of religion altogether."[3] So what is at stake is the *kind* of religion presented in music that is easy, trivial, light, inconsequential, mundane, or everyday. The very existence of the expression *sacred music* once conveyed the notion that some music was different from other music, *intentionally* different, different precisely because it was devoted to a sacred (not common) cause.

To give a hymnic example, let us consider "O Sacred Head, Now Wounded." Attributed to Bernard of Clairvaux (c. 1153), this passion hymn was translated into German by the Lutheran

have such realities as "shock radio," for instance. But only if the culture became profoundly refined would there be a commercial return to refined music. This, to date, has not happened.

3. *Amusing Ourselves to Death: Public Discourse in the Age of Television* (New York: Viking, 1985), 121.

hymn-writer Paul Gerhardt (1656), and then into English by James Waddell Alexander (one of the Princeton Alexanders) in 1830. Its very age, and translation into multiple languages, proves that it is deemed to have significant merit as a hymn. Consider a verse such as this:

> What thou, my Lord, hast suffered was all for sinners' gain:
> Mine, mine was the transgression, but thine the deadly pain.
> Lo, here I fall, my Savior! 'Tis I deserve thy place;
> Look on me with thy favor, vouchsafe to me thy grace.

As should be the case with passion hymns, this one deals with the gravity of the crucifixion: the awful and remarkable reality of the God-Man dying for sinful humans to live. Such a hymn requires a somber musical setting; to set such a hymn to a trivial, light tune would be not only musically self-defeating and disharmonious, but also sacrilegious.

One very important qualification needs to be made when discussing meta-messages. When we say that certain forms "send" the wrong message, we do not mean that everyone who "receives" the message actually *receives* that wrong message.[4] Some people might receive a message differently from others. Some people, when hearing sacred music produced in banal musical form, find nothing banal about it. So when we say that such forms send the wrong meta-message, we are not saying that every single recipient of those forms receives them that way.

---

4. Literary critics refer to this phenomenon as the *affective fallacy*, an expression first coined, if I am not mistaken, in the significant work of William Kurtz Wimsatt and Monroe C. Beardsley, *The Verbal Icon: Studies in the Meaning of Poetry*, chap. 1 (Lexington: University Press of Kentucky, 1954), 21ff.

Let me illustrate. A friend of mine likes Frank Sinatra's music. I do, too, considering Sinatra to have been one of the best "lounge lizards" of all time. Like my father before me, however, I find that some of Sinatra's music makes me cringe because he had extraordinary difficulty with pitch. To Sinatra, pitch was apparently a fairly elusive concept. Sometimes he's on pitch; other times, he's off just enough to make me cringe. But my friend, whose pitch is not very acute, doesn't notice this. When my friend sings, he is not entirely tone-deaf. His notes rise when they ought to rise, and fall when they ought to fall, so he has some concept of pitch, but it is fairly imperfect. He says he's never heard a Sinatra song that made him cringe. Does this mean that Sinatra's pitch was good, or does it mean that my friend's ears are not sufficiently discriminating to hear that Sinatra's pitch was off? I think we know the answer.

So also, there are many people in our culture whose musical listening has been almost exclusively banal; 98 percent or more of the music they have heard has been pop. To their ears, this is just what music sounds like; they haven't heard enough significant music to distinguish significant music from insignificant music. On the rare occasion that they have heard significant music, it has seemed foreign to them, as Oriental music seems foreign to me. Therefore, when I suggest that the meta-message of most contemporary worship music is trivial, I get deer-in-the-headlights looks from such individuals, because it doesn't sound particularly trivial to them. But I suggest that it does send a message of triviality, even if not everyone receives the message that way. In terms of the properties that music has, and the options available to composers, the choices made in composing most contemporary worship music have the qualities associated with comparatively trivial forms of music. My friend does not hear when Sinatra is off-pitch—but Sinatra *is* off-pitch. And my contemporary worship music friends do not hear the banal or trivial in contemporary worship music—but it often *is* trivial.

Some proponents of contemporary worship music wish to dismiss such meta-message considerations, but they can do so only by overlooking their own practices and those of their leaders. Take the Sunday attire of Pastor Rick Warren of Saddleback Church, for example. He famously does not wear a starched white dress shirt, with a tie and a business suit. He wears an open-collared, casual shirt.[5] Now, if this happened merely once, we might think that he had spilled coffee on his dress shirt while en route to church, and had to grab whatever he could so that the show could go on. But he wears this kind of shirt every time, so it is obviously a self-conscious, deliberate choice. Pastor Warren *knows* that wearing an open-collared, casual shirt sends a meta-message, one that he hopes will communicate things such as approachableness and nonjudgmentalism.

Indeed, one of my acquaintances who models much of his own ministry after Saddleback Church told me excitedly some years ago that he had that very year had

---

5. With some exceptions. When speaking at a presidential inaugural, Pastor Warren wears a dress shirt and a tie. Why? Is the inauguration of an American president more important than the celebration of the resurrection of Christ? Is President Obama more important than the King of kings? I don't fault Pastor Warren for the wardrobe change; it is entirely likely that President Obama's protocol people gave precise instructions to Pastor Warren regarding wardrobe.

a "breakthrough" in his ministry. When I, pastoring at the time myself, asked what constituted the breakthrough, he informed me that he no longer wore a suit and tie on Sunday. I'm willing to let history decide how much of a breakthrough this really was, or even whether it was one at all. My point is merely this: my friend was very much aware that this was a *significant* choice, and significant precisely because of the meta-message sent by that choice. Therefore, meta-message considerations cannot be simply dismissed; they are fair game for honest (and charitable, one hopes) discussion. And if the culture observers are correct, the meta-message that contemporary music sends is this: Nothing is important; everything is just amusing or entertaining. This is hardly a Christian message.

Questions for Reflection

1. What is a *meta-message*?
2. Can meta-messages disagree with verbal messages? If so, how?
3. What relation exists between commerce and pop culture? Why does commerce desire pop culture to be accessible? Why does commerce wish to avoid music that requires a steep learning curve to appreciate?
4. If pop music is essentially trivial or ephemeral, do you think it is an apt vehicle for worshiping an everlasting and holy God?
5. Discuss Neil Postman's comment: "I believe I am not mistaken in saying that Christianity is a demanding and

serious religion. When it is delivered as easy and amusing, it is another kind of religion altogether."

6. When Pastor Rick Warren wears an open-collared shirt to church, what meta-message is he intending to send? What is one instance in which he seems to be sending a different meta-message? Why?

5

SACRED MUSIC?

IN SOME PLACES in our culture, people still occasionally speak about *sacred music*, and indeed there are theological seminaries that offer courses of study in sacred music.[1] But the term is in the process of disappearing. Why? Because sacred music in our day does not wish to sound different from secular music; to the contrary, it intentionally emulates it, and attempts to sound exactly like it. But if worship is a sacred task, what is wrong with the musical aspects of worship sounding sacred?

Defenders of contemporary worship music quite commonly make statements to this effect: "This is just a matter of style. We like our kind of music, and older people like their kind of music." But traditional sacred music is *not* older people's "kind of music." My father's generation was the first generation to experience pop/mass culture, and the music of his generation was primarily big band. The hymns he grew up with were not rewritten in a big-band idiom. Similarly, my generation (whose

1. Acquaintances of mine who teach music lament that at some such seminaries, however, there are few requirements in the areas of aesthetic theory or even serious musical theory. Such schools are apparently performance-oriented, teaching their students how to perform what the students select, but doing little, if anything, to train them in any coherent theory of sacred music.

iconic group The Who performed "My Generation") has had its own idiom, rock. But we didn't rewrite the hymns in a rock idiom. More importantly, we do not listen to hymn-styled music in our leisure time. That is, traditional worship forms are not, in fact, our preferred musical style when we listen to music. Such traditional forms are not "our" music; they are the *church's* music, and they antedate us by many generations. Our approval of them, in worship, is not due to the fact that they are "our" music, the music we listen to in our leisure time. Our approval of them is due (in part) to the fact that they are the *church's* music, and ours only insofar as we are part of that holy catholic church.

It is the defenders of contemporary worship music whose worship music emulates "their music" in their leisure time. In leisure time, they listen to guitar music; in worship, they listen to guitar music. In leisure time, they listen to pop music; in worship, they listen to pop music. In leisure time, they listen to music written for a small ensemble; in worship, they listen to music written for a small ensemble. Since this is in fact what they do, it is not entirely surprising that they project this practice onto others, and suggest that others are doing what they are doing. But as a matter of fact, it is not so. They alone are suggesting that worship music must conform (or ordinarily ought to conform) to the same standards as their leisure music; no one else has ever suggested or done this.

The concept of sacred music is not one that should be dismissed lightly or without serious reflection. The attempt of those who have historically devoted themselves to it has been to create music suitable to that remarkable occasion in life when the creature meets the Creator, when the mortal meets the immortal, when, yes, the temporal meets the eternal, when time meets eternity. Whether consciously or not, I suspect the one criterion that every one of these individuals has rejected right off the bat was and is contemporaneity. The one thing that sacred music cannot do is to omit the divine, and the divine is eternal, timeless, without beginning or end, the Alpha and the Omega. In terms of form, then, contemporary music might be very appropriate for meetings between temporal beings, but is it appropriate for an immortal God meeting beings who, by Christ's power to resurrect, will one day be immortal themselves? Note the way in which this rhetorical question is raised: the question is not whether it is *lawful* to employ a contemporary form; the question is whether it is *appropriate*.

I am reminded of Neil Postman's story of two priests who debated one night whether it was appropriate to pray and smoke cigars at the same time. Each wrote to the Pope to have the matter resolved, and it appeared that His Holiness gave contradictory advice. One priest had asked, "Is it right to smoke while praying?" to which the Pope said, "No." But the other had asked, "Is it right to pray while smoking?" to which the Pope said, "Yes." Following this advice myself, I occasionally find myself praying while smoking a cigar; but I don't think it would be appropriate to distribute cigars with bulletins at the entrance to the church on Sunday morning, and to invite people to light them up during worship. I doubt that anyone could demonstrate that the practice of cigar-smoking is unlawful; but many could demonstrate that it is not appropriate to the setting of corporate worship.[2]

2. This is where Professor John Frame and I tend to have our occasional disagreements. In his desire to have the same principles govern worship that govern "all of life," it appears to me either that it is *always* unlawful to smoke cigars or that, if it is lawful

Contemporary worship music deliberately attempts to sound like the music we hear every day in the culture around us. It goes out of its way *not* to sound foreign or different. But if meeting our Maker and Redeemer is different from all our other meetings, why shouldn't the various aspects of that meeting be different from the aspects of other meetings? If God is "wholly other" than we, why would a meeting with him look as though he were "wholly like" us? If he is holy, why shouldn't the language we use when we approach him be holy? If he is sacred, why should we not attempt to construct music that sounds sacred, rather than profane? Why should the category of *sacred music* disappear?

Questions for Reflection

1. Did my father's generation insist that the church reset her worship music in the idiom of the big-band style of his generation's pop music? Why or why not?
2. Should use of the expression (and the reality of) *sacred music* be retained or discontinued? Why?
3. If the antonymn to *sacred* is *mundane* (or *profane*), should worship music be sacred, or should it be mundane, and why?

---

to smoke them, we could do so in worship. By my reasoning, worship is a profoundly different occasion from other occasions, and must be governed by different principles and considerations from those that direct us on other occasions (and so, ironically, I smoke cigars but do not permit them in worship; Professor Frame does not smoke them but, on his principles, might approve them in worship). But the point is not insignificant. If Professor Frame and I differ at such a fundamental level, it is not surprising at all that at a less fundamental level (which musical principles to employ in sacred music) we would have some degree of disagreement also.

6

THREE MUSICAL GENRES

IN HIS *All God's Children and Blue Suede Shoes,*[1] Ken Myers has asserted
that in our culture, music (and other art) tends to fall into
three categories: high/classical music, folk music, and pop/
mass music. His book consists of descriptions of the characteristic traits of these different artistic idioms, and I will
briefly summarize them here. Readers interested in the matter
are encouraged to read the book in its entirety, however, since
the following summary abbreviates profoundly and cannot do
justice to the careful analysis that Myers has provided. I will
briefly summarize Myers's thoughts in each genre (though the
illustrations are clumsily mine) before discussing what I believe
this means for contemporary worship music. An appendix to
this book contains Myers's two-column comparison of the
tendencies of classical culture and pop culture.

High/Classical Culture

In high/classical culture, the compositional choices
made by the artist emphasize realities that are transcendent,

1. Westchester, IL: Crossway Books, 1989.

multigenerational, significant, communal, and less accessible. The classical composer intends to suggest the existence of transcendent, not merely immanent, reality. Myth and religion are common themes of lyrical music in this genre, and even in its nonlyrical expressions, the genre suggests the possibility of that which transcends our merely mundane state. Indeed, one of the first treatises ever written on aesthetic theory was that of Longinus, entitled *On the Sublime*. The classical tradition, while carrying on many debates about aesthetic theory, still tends to embrace the notion that music might be particularly suited to communicating the sublime or transcendent to us, in a way separately from language, which is perhaps too limited and limiting. When we listen to Claude Debussy's *Prelude to "The Afternoon of a Faun,"* for instance, we don't necessarily think about fauns or afternoons, but the floating, pulsing, enticing quality of the music invites us beyond the mundane to an experience of reality itself that might float above us or entice us beyond our mundane existence.

High/classical culture is also self-consciously multigenerational. While a composer wishes to find some appreciative listeners in his own generation, his goal is to find what is comparatively "timeless" in music, and his desire is to please many subsequent generations of listeners. Indeed, whenever an artist achieves this multigenerational success, we tend to refer to his work as a *classic*, for this reason. The *Mona Lisa* is perhaps not less intriguing today than it was in the sixteenth century or the centuries that intervened. When I first listened seriously to Ludwig van Beethoven's Seventh Symphony some years ago, I found myself curiously entranced by the second movement, and didn't even tell anyone, because I thought certainly there's no reason to be so charmed by the Andante movement. Imagine my relief when I discovered later that at its original performances in 1813, the audience requested the second movement for the encore, and that indeed this movement was so popular that it was sometimes later employed as a substitute for the second movement of the Eighth. I'm not a musician, so I cannot explain what it is in Beethoven that so connected to audiences of the early nineteenth century and to listeners two centuries later. I do know this: Beethoven discovered something about the essence or power of music in that piece that transcended a single generation.

High/classical culture also deals with matters that are significant, even in its nonlyrical compositions. This is not to deny that there is some range, nor to deny that Franz Joseph Haydn, for instance, often produced music that had a playful tone. But as a genre, this idiom suggests significance. Listen to Johann Sebastian Bach's Toccata and Fugue in D Minor, for instance, and whether you like the piece or not, its gravity is unmistakable, as is the case with his Passacaglia and Fugue in C Minor, even if the latter seems a tad less driven than the former. If a child took no pleasure in Bach's compositions, for instance, this would have neither bothered nor deterred Bach at all. He knew his work was too serious for a child to appreciate, and he was content if serious listeners took pleasure in his work.

High/classical culture is also communal; it celebrates our common experience as humans, rather than our particular experience as individuals. When Johannes Brahms wrote his *Ein deutsches Requiem*, for instance, it was neither an expression of merely his own personal grief over the loss of Robert Schumann (who died about the time he began the work) nor an expression of merely his own personal grief over the loss of his mother (who died about the time the work was finished, seven years later). Rather, at a minimum, it was and is, as its name affirms, a *German* requiem, and appreciative listeners consider it a *human* requiem, a musical work that feels grief more acutely than most requiems do, and yet offers compassionate, even tender, consolations to those who grieve. That is, Brahms composes as a griever-among-grievers, not as a solitary griever. The frequent use of folk music in the classical literature of the nineteenth and early twentieth centuries reflected this sense of communal identity, rather than merely or primarily individual identity.

High/classical culture is also comparatively less accessible than other artistic idioms. In order to attain its other ends, this genre requires a certain learning curve. While anyone can hum along with "Three Blind Mice," not everyone will immediately gravitate to a Brahms quintet for strings and piano. While all are invited to find the transcendent, sublime pleasures of classical music, the classical composer does not write "for the masses," nor does he care greatly what they think of his work.

There are other characteristics of high/classical culture. Typically, it is fairly restrained or disciplined—for instance, trying to achieve certain formal goals. Brahms scoured used bookstores for old scores by Dietrich Buxtehude and J. S. Bach, for example, in his quest to master musical form. And he somewhat famously remarked, "While my music cannot always be beautiful, it must always be perfect."[2] Such formal perfection requires

2. Brahms's precise words were actually, "There is not a note too much or too little, not a bar you could improve on. Whether it is also *beautiful* is an entirely different matter, but perfect it *must* be." Jan Swafford, *Johannes Brahms: A Biography* (New York: Vintage,

years of study, and many hours of editing and correcting initial drafts of scores. Such music is the opposite of the in-your-face, volume-cranked-up guitar playing of Led Zeppelin, for instance.[3] Indeed, Brahms himself was an extremely private individual who never married, with only a small circle of close friends, most of whom, like Clara Schumann, found him exasperating. Just as he rarely exposed himself to intimates, so also his music shows remarkable restraint in its expressions of passion. Many people find it difficult to acquire a taste for Brahms, I think, for precisely this reason—that his work is emotionally restrained (and often gloomy when not restrained).

For our purposes, however, note how well suited this genre is for the interests of the Christian religion, whose emphases are similarly transcendent, multigenerational, significant, communal, and less accessible. Revivalists, populists, and evangelicals may resist this last criterion (less accessible), but they do so only until they read and understand Jesus' discussion of the "narrow" way that leads to life, and his sober commentary that "those who find it are few" (Matt. 7:14). We hardly expect a redemptive religion ever to be more inclusive than what Paul found it to be: a stumbling block to most Jews and folly to most Gentiles (1 Cor. 1:23).

Folk Culture

Folk culture, according to Myers, is transcendent, multi-generational, significant, communal, yet more accessible than classical/high culture. Without repeating what was said above

---

1997), 46, quoting George Henschel, *Personal Recollections of Johannes Brahms: Some of His Letters to and Pages from a Journal Kept by George Henschel* (Boston: Gorham, 1907), 39.

3. Though even here, Jimmy Page worked very hard in practice to make his guitar riffs appear to be more spontaneous than they actually were.

about high/classical culture, we note that folk culture shares many of its qualities. It deals with transcendent reality, calling us away from the merely mundane. It is self-consciously multigenerational because it exists, in large measure, as a means of handing down a given tradition from one generation to another, lest a given subculture lose its self-identity. And while it is not as universally communal as high/classical art, it is communal, self-consciously so, as opposed to being individual. Indeed, it was fairly easy for classical composers such as Antonín Dvořák (*New World Symphony*), Johannes Brahms (*Hungarian Dances*), and Aaron Copland (*Appalachian Spring*) to incorporate folk idioms into their work because they were not so different on these points.

Folk culture, however, is more accessible than classical culture. In order to be passed on from generation to generation, its forms had to be accessible to the group as a whole, and not the provenance of a special few. So most folk idioms, once one "gets the hang" of them, do not require the learning curve associated with classical forms. They are thus very suitable for Christian hymnody, and we recognize their presence in such hymns as "Be Thou My Vision" (SLANE, Irish), "Now Blessed Be the Lord Our God" (McKEE, American Spiritual), and "Let Us with a Gladsome Mind" (INNOCENTS, French).

African-Americans face an interesting challenge at this moment in history. In the American experiment, the folk idiom of the spiritual was developed in this tradition, as a means of understanding (and, perhaps, enduring) the horrible reality of slavery within a Christian framework. The extreme pathos, combined with faith, makes this genre unique. Yet the genre may disappear because some African-Americans object to the genre, believing that it implicitly "justified" the practice of slavery by providing a theological ground for tolerating or enduring it. So for some, while the genre serves the purpose of connecting them to their undeniably difficult past, for others it disserves the greater community because of its associations with justifying submission to the slave trade. Outsiders to the tradition, such as I, are obviously unqualified to render an opinion about whether the genre should survive or not. But I do observe that it shares the qualities of other folk genres: it deals with significant, transcendent realities, and is deliberately pangenerational, yet is more accessible than classical/high idioms.

Other such folk idioms still remain, but have become largely marginalized in our culture. If classical-music radio stations are comparatively rare (and commercially unsuccessful), folk-music radio stations probably do not even exist.[4] The ballad, for instance, as a folk genre has all but disappeared. On occasion it appears, and some pop artists even know how to employ it skillfully (if commercially riskily). When Eric Clapton's son fell to his death, for instance, and Clapton wrestled with the question of how to memorialize his son appropriately, he skillfully employed a folk idiom, the ballad, when he wrote "No Tears in Heaven." Clapton did not employ the more typical rocking pop style for which he is largely known—because the ephemeral, fleeting, trivial nature of the idiom was incompatible with his purpose. But the ballad form has room for what is significant; and as an expression of human grief, it can be passed along from one generation to another, since grief is a universal, pangenerational reality. While every particular grief is exquisitely personal, and therefore unique, grief itself in a

4. And if my colleague Joshua Drake is right, they could not exist, since folk music is essentially participatory and was never intended as performance music.

mortal world is universal. Clapton elected to employ a musical genre (the folk ballad) that permitted him to express what was both intensely personal *and* intensely universal, what is deeply felt and universally experienced. Johannes Brahms composed his *Ein deutsches Requiem* to address the shared reality of human grief, not merely his own experience of it. Clapton also wrote his own kind of requiem, which he shared with a human tradition that shares the experience of grief.

Observers of contemporary pop music, such as John McWhorter, Ken Myers, Todd Gitlin, David Denby, and Martha Bayles, have observed how individualistic (noncorporate or noncommunal) it is, in contrast to the communal nature of classical and folk idioms. Only Clapton performs "Layla"; only Led Zeppelin performs "Black Dog"; only ZZ Top performs "La Grange"; only Michael Jackson performed "Billie Jean"; and, thankfully, only Pink got a party started. That is, pop is an art form that showcases the particular, individual (idiosyncratic?) *performance* of a work rather than the work itself. These observers have noted how different this phenomenon is from the music of the 1930s and 1940s, when many different commercial artists performed essentially the same repertoire of music. Tommy Dorsey, Duke Ellington, and Glenn Miller performed many of the same works. While the Benny Goodman/Gene Krupa/Harry James instrumental version of Louis Prima's 1936 "Sing, Sing, Sing" was (justifiably) famous, others played and recorded it also. This practice was common in their era because each particular piece of music *itself* was celebrated, not the piece's idiosyncratic individual performance.[5] And of

5. In 1939, for example, Harold Arlen and E. Y. Harburg published "Over the Rainbow," made famous by Judy Garland. More than fifty other artists have made

course, it hardly needs to be observed that classical music is known for the music itself far more than for its particular performances. Some knowledgeable people are able to distinguish Wilhelm Furtwängler's recordings of Beethoven from those of Herbert von Karajan, but the fact that many conductors perform Beethoven proves the point. Note, then, that some musical idioms celebrate music that "belongs" to the culture (or subculture) at large, not to its particular performer. Many hymns and hymn tunes are anonymous: they do not belong to any particular artist; they belong to the church.

One could plausibly argue that the folk idiom is in fact the most appropriate idiom for Christian hymnody, and indeed argue that Christian hymnody, historically considered, *is* a folk idiom. It is a subculture's way of transmitting its heritage and tradition from one generation to another. Hymnody was and is to the Christian church in general what the Negro spiritual was to African-Americans in the seventeenth to nineteenth centuries. It is a genre that is, on the one hand, transcendent, corporate (as opposed to individual), and multigenerational like classical music, but accessible to the masses like pop music.

Pop/Mass Culture

According to Ken Myers, the sensibilities promoted by pop/mass culture are immanent, monogenerational, banal,

---

recordings of this piece, including Glenn Miller, Harry Nilsson, Placido Domingo, Patti LaBelle, Liberace, Dizzy Gillespie, Kenny G, Ella Fitzgerald, Johnny Mathis, Sarah Vaughan, Billy Ray Cyrus, Carly Simon, Little Anthony, Dave Brubeck, Eric Clapton, Barbra Streisand, Livingston Taylor, Ray Charles, the Mormon Tabernacle Choir, Willie Nelson, Harry Connick Jr., Stan Getz, Maynard Ferguson, Chet Baker, Chet Atkins, Frank Sinatra, Sandi Patty, Melissa Manchester, George Fenton, Olivia Newton-John, and Kaulana Kanekoa.

individualistic, accessible. In almost every way possible, the sensibilities of pop culture differ from those of classical and folk. It is immanent in the sense that it celebrates the present moment and situation, divorced from past and future, and lives viscerally in that moment. It surrounds itself with guitars, for instance, because the guitar has become the musical "voice" of a particular place in a particular time. Pop culture is self-consciously and intentionally monogenerational; it intends to sound novel, and views itself as artistically pioneering.

The sensibilities of pop culture are also individualistic, rather than communal. Rarely does more than one artist perform a given piece of music, because each individual artist puts his or her own individual self into the performance. By contrast, many orchestras have played the Brahms Fourth Symphony, and while The Cleveland Orchestra, for instance, may have its own distinctive approach, the essence is substantially Brahms. Thus, pop culture celebrates individual self-expression and experience at the expense of community expression and experience.

But this celebration of the individual ultimately separates the self from community. As Herbert Schlossberg says: "The cult of self-expression, with all its excrescences, has become so pervasive that society itself is often said to have fallen into narcissism. The individual believes himself to be the measure of both reality and moral principle.... As Harvard's Irving Babbitt put it in an earlier period, 'every ass that's romantic thinks he's inspired.'"[6]

6. *Idols for Destruction: The Conflict of Christian Faith and American Culture* (Wheaton, IL: Crossway, 1993), 166–67. Cf. also the earlier, significant study by Christopher Lasch, *The Culture of Narcissism: American Life in an Age of Diminishing Expectations* (New York: Norton, 1978). For the effects of such narcissism on pop music, see John H. McWhorter, *Doing Our Own Thing: The Degradation of Language and Music and Why We Should, Like, Care* (New York: Gotham, 2003).

For commercial reasons, pop culture must be both banal and accessible. Pop culture is mass culture is commercial culture. Pop culture exists as the child of two parents: mass media and commercial forces. Insofar as the term means anything, *pop* means "aimed at the population at large." Using mass media (initially radio, but extending and expanding through today's electronic media), the population as a whole can be targeted. Early on, commercial forces understood the extraordinary economic potential of sending commercial broadcasts that reached large segments of the population. Realizing, however, that people would not tune in radios or televisions to commercial messages alone, the commercial forces needed to produce "programming," something other than commercial messages that could capture people's attention, so that commercials could be interwoven with it.

This is why pop culture must be accessible. If it is difficult or off-putting, people will change channels or stations to find something easier to watch or listen to. Pop culture, therefore, must not require a demanding learning curve; it must be almost instantly accessible. High/classical art strives to produce what is enduringly beautiful, even if some effort must be expended to appreciate it; pop art does not have this luxury. The commercial forces that drive it cannot afford to lose audiences. Proof of this today is that virtually no classical-radio stations survive commercially; they must be funded by private and corporate grants and gifts, and through other fund-raising efforts. Such stations do not reach the population at large because their programming is difficult, requiring some effort and patience to appreciate. Pop music, by contrast, is easily accessible, and therefore commercially viable.

Pop culture sometimes blends with folk culture, as has happened with so-called country music in the last two decades. Increasingly, country music has adjusted its hard original edge into the more accessible sounds associated with pop music. When the NFL, for instance, apparently had some sort of contract dispute with Pink (who covered Joan Jett to perform the opening music in its initial season of *Sunday Night Football*), they had no trouble finding a country-music star, Faith Hill, who would perform the same song in subsequent seasons. Country music is now merely pop music with a mildly Southern accent; it is no longer what it was thirty years ago.[7] Of course, country musicians are now wealthy because they have learned to make their music more accessible, less distinct, less demanding, less off-putting.

In the process of producing art that is easily accessible, of course, pop music is necessarily banal or trivial. That is, in producing easily accessible art that requires no learning curve, it necessarily avoids and evades those musical properties that are more demanding on the listener. But these properties are the very ones that permit music to transcend the commonplace and aspire to the sublime. Oddly enough, even the term *music* is derivative of a Greek adjective that means, etymologically, "produced by the Muse." In Greek, then, music is a gift from part of the Greco-Roman pantheon, a semi-divine creation. Our verb *muse*, therefore, etymologically meant "to give careful attention to a matter," as though it were produced by the semi-

7. The Rev. Charles Wingard, of Huntsville, Alabama, informs me that authentic country music still exists on stations such as WQAH, 105.7, in Hartselle, Alabama. The station's resistance to conformity to the mores of pop culture may be revealed in its advertising of events such as the Double Springs, Alabama "Women's Skillet Tossin' Competition."

divine Muse. The word *a-muse*, then, means just the opposite: "no-muse," or "no serious attention to be given." A-musement thus puts the divinity in the background—what an oxymoron: *background music!*—because our pop music may be amusing, but it is surely not sublime.

But now, as we wrestle with form and content issues, note how the sensibilities of pop culture clash with those of Christianity. The Christian religion is old, like it or not. It is not a new thing: it is two thousand years old in its current form, and its roots in the religion of Abraham and Moses go back almost another two thousand years. And it will continue to be here until history concludes at the return of Christ. Christianity is not monogenerational, nor is it monocultural; it transcends generations and particular cultures as a global religion. Similarly, it is communal, not individual. We once confessed belief in "the holy catholic church, the communion of saints," but this would require acknowledging the existence of a many-generational communion of followers of Christ. As our athletes remind us: "There is no *I* in *team.*"

Surely Christianity is transcendent, not immanent. It teaches us, if anything, that there is Something, indeed Someone, beyond us, and beyond our entire universe. It functions to draw us out of self-love to love for neighbor and for God. It is most certainly not "all about you." And Christianity is not accessible, in the ordinary sense of the word. It does not exist for our amusement or entertainment; it challenges us to forsake a broad way and embrace a narrow one; it calls us to repent of and forsake our current values and habits; it demands that we take up a cross and bear it daily. It surely is not trivial; there is nothing trite or insignificant about part of the Godhead's becoming incarnate to die for sinners. None of this stern, transcendent seriousness is consistent with the values of pop culture. The sensibilities of pop culture and those of Christianity are almost entirely opposed to each other, and when we attempt to force Christianity into the constraints of an individual-affirming, consumerist, monogenerational, immanentistic genre, it simply won't fit. Inevitably, the content is shaped by the form into which it is put, and the message becomes a casual, consumerist "Hey, what do you think about this?" rather than a call to "repentance that leads to life" (Acts 11:18).

In fact, for those who promote contemporary worship music, there tends to be an impatience even with this present discussion, because for them, "Hey, why fight about something like this— it's only music, after all." *Mad* magazine's Alfred E. Neuman is the poster boy for such a culture: "What? Me worry?" But such an attitude is precisely that of the dehumanized, trivial, ironic posture of our pop culture: nothing is really serious, nothing is really significant. Everything is just a consumerist choice; I like my choice, and you like yours.

Questions for Reflection

1. What are the characteristics of classical art and music?
2. What are the characteristics of folk art and music?
3. What are the characteristics of pop art and music?
4. Which of these genres has the steepest learning curve and is therefore less accessible than the others? Which has the least steep curve? Explain.
5. Which of these genres (may be more than one) is multi-generational? Explain.

6. Which of these genres (may be more than one) is communal/corporate rather than individual? Explain.
7. Which of these genres is most restrained/disciplined; which is least restrained/disciplined? Explain.
8. How, if at all, do the properties of these particular genres of music make them more appropriate or less appropriate to worship song?

7

MUSICAL QUESTIONS

Aaron Copland's Five Components

In Aaron Copland's book on music appreciation,[1] he suggested that music has five properties: rhythm, melody, harmony, timbre, and form; and he suggested that one's ability to take pleasure in music depended on the ability to notice these various properties, and the skillful choices composers make of them. There are other ways of talking about the matter, and it is even possible that one could add to the list (e.g., is tone or mood merely an effect of these, or is it a separate thing to listen for?). But Copland's five categories are, at a minimum, a starting place for talking about what traits might make a given musical work more or less appropriate for a worship setting. Some rhythmical patterns, for instance, while aesthetically interesting or pleasing, might be beyond the ability of a typical congregation to sing. Consider, as an obvious example, the opening measures of Igor Stravinsky's *The Rite of Spring*, in which three different

---

1. Aaron Copland, *What to Listen For in Music* (New York: McGraw-Hill, 1939).

time signatures overlie each other. Whatever aesthetic value there is in such an experiment (and I affirm that there is), it would be virtually impossible to try to put together a hymn that followed this rhythmic pattern. Congregations would simply find it unsingable.

Similarly, if a congregation thinks there may be theological significance to singing in harmony, some hymns have better oblique parts written for them than others (contrast the bass and tenor lines in various renditions of the tune HYFRYDOL, for instance). In some hymnals, the tenor lines are notoriously dull; in others they add substantial interest to the work. The key signature in which a hymn is written is significant; often a hymn is pitched a step or two higher than the average voice can comfortably sing. If we wish the congregation to participate, the hymn should be pitched in a singable key. Similarly, when a hymn is put to more than one tune, some of those tunes are more singable than others, and it is wiser to select the more singable tune (provided that it suits the text).

Timbre is an extremely important consideration for the accompanying instruments, just as it is a significant component of music per se. Brass is conspicuously and necessarily absent in the beautiful, haunting opening of the first movement ("*Selig sind, die da Leid tragen*" ["blessed are they who mourn"]) of the Brahms *Requiem*, for instance, because its martial timbre would be inappropriate to the tone that Brahms wished to achieve there. But then the brass almost jump off the stage in the transitional part of the second movement, where Brahms contrasts all flesh, which withers like grass or fades like the flower, with "the Word of our God [which] will stand forever."

In this second movement, the pensive first part is altogether strings and woodwinds, whose timbres themselves suggest ephemerality, therefore perfectly suiting the text, which says, "The grass withers, and the flower fades, when the breath of the Lord blows on it." But then Isaiah contrasts this fading creature (earlier likened to humans) with the eternal Word of the eternal God, and the percussive and brass instruments shout out in a strong triple forte. Timbre, then, is a very significant musical component, which skilled composers employ quite deliberately.

Why is it the case, for instance, that not all music can be transposed from one instrument to another?[2] Why do we not transpose Pyotr Il'yich Tchaikovsky's (or Edward Elgar's or Antonín Dvořák's) *Serenade for Strings*? The answer is somewhat obvious: assuming that Tchaikovsky knew what he was doing, his *Serenade for Strings* made skillful use of stringed instruments, and would not be musically successful if transposed for brass, for instance. Indeed, one of the most significant changes in symphonic music in the twentieth century was the increased use of the brass and percussion sections of the symphony.

So what are the peculiar properties of the acoustic (or electric) guitar? What distinguishes the timbre of the guitar from the timbre of other instruments, and does this distinctive trait suit the guitar well to accompany a chorus (and a congregation is a chorus)? Well, I'm not musician enough to know all the details of this answer, but I know this: in the classical field, few choral pieces have been written for guitar accompaniment.

2. Skilled musicians can indeed make some transpositions. Many readers are familiar with Samuel Barber's *Adagio for Strings*, and some are also familiar with his own wonderful transposition of this piece for chorus in his *Agnus Dei*.

Apparently, the people who know more about music than I do have decided that the guitar is better suited to smaller ensembles: duets, trios, quartets, and especially solos.

Further, what are the peculiar properties of the timbre of the guitar, in terms of what lyrics and messages it can accompany? If Brahms chose not to use brass for the first part of his first movement, and if he did choose brass for the second part, was he musically incompetent? Did he not know what he was doing? Of course he did. So we raise the question: what kind of theological or religious content requires, or even survives, accompaniment by guitar?

The guitar is not a new instrument. Why have classical musicians not frequently employed it to accompany choral music, and why have our better-known sacred musicians, from J. S. Bach onward, not written sacred music for it? I'm not a musician, so I don't know the answer to that question, but I suspect that the guitar just can't do it well.[3] The guitar's timbre limits it to less significant things; it is like Tom Cruise standing in the courtroom before Jack Nicholson, who says: "You can't handle the truth." Maybe the guitar can handle a little truth, but it can't handle much.[4]

3. One limitation of the guitar is the strumming motion itself, and the rhythms created by that motion, rhythms that often conflict with the rhythms of the accompanying parts (alto, tenor, bass). Such rhythms prevent the singing of parts. Some churches choose to limit themselves to singing in unison and deliberately choose not to permit the singing of parts. But those that do not object to the singing of parts, or those that encourage it, as a reflection of the church's harmonious unity, ought to recognize that when the guitar accompanies, the other parts ordinarily cannot be sung. Related to this is the tendency for contemporary worship music not to be attended by written music with written parts. Will this not discourage musical literacy and the singing of harmony? And do we wish to discourage such things without some serious discussion first?

4. My very good colleague Stan Keehlwetter, Dean of the Chapel at our college, occasionally reminds us that there is *always* at least one "traditional hymn" in our chapel services; and

At any rate, contemporary worship music, while ordinarily professing to be aesthetically relativistic, has one absolute: Thou shalt play the guitar. This is the one nonnegotiable of contemporary worship music; worship music absolutely *must* be accompanied on the guitar. It is somewhat ironic that people who claim that aesthetics are merely subjective and relativistic are so inflexible on this point, whereas traditional sacred music has been just the opposite. Traditional sacred music has claimed that aesthetics *are* objective and absolute, but has *not* claimed that only one instrument can be employed to accompany the singing of praise. There is no good musical reason to insist on accompanying congregational song with a guitar; it is poorly suited to the task, and it profoundly limits the other choices that can be made once it is chosen. We simply cannot accompany Martin Luther's "A Mighty Fortress Is Our God" successfully with a guitar.[5]

Corporate Music versus Private Music

An accompanying instrument, one that accompanies choral singing, has different demands from a solo instrument, or an

---

I occasionally remark that there is *never* one "traditional hymn" in our chapel services—and we are both right. Dr. Keehlwetter is right that the *lyrics* of at least one traditional hymn are always employed; and I am right that the musical *setting* is never traditional. So the question is whether the instrumental and rhythmic dimensions are or are not part of a hymn. For him they are not; for me (and, I suspect, for musical composers) they are.

5. Some years ago, my former colleague David Wells told me of an encounter with a student at the photocopier. David was copying a draft of a chapter of his *Above All Earthly Pow'rs: Christ in a Postmodern World* (Grand Rapids: Eerdmans, 2005), and the student found the title interesting. David told her it was from Luther's hymn, and she asked, "What hymn?" David told her it was from "A Mighty Fortress Is Our God," and she replied that she was not familiar with that hymn. Imagine a student at a theological seminary who has never heard "A Mighty Fortress"! How do we account for such remarkable ignorance? Luther's hymn cannot be accompanied by a guitar, and therefore the hapless young woman had never heard it.

instrument that accompanies an individual voice or two. The guitar is nearly hopeless for accompanying a chorus; opera is rarely (if ever) accompanied by a guitar. Because the guitar is strummed, it is far more at home with duple meters than triple meters, and its resonance is such that, if amplified, it has similar liabilities to those of the organ: when loud enough to provide tempo and pitch, it tends to drown out the lyrics. The guitar accompanies a single voice, or a duet or trio, very well (hence its use in folk music); but it simply does not have the percussive properties of a piano, for instance, which strikes the strings and then the sound falls away.

The prime virtue in accompanying instruments, therefore, is to fulfill the purpose of accompaniment (at a minimum, to help maintain pitch and tempo), and one test of the adequacy of such an instrument is to ask whether it facilitates singing a broad or narrow range of music. Try singing "A Mighty Fortress Is Our God" to the EIN' FESTE BURG melody with guitar, and you will realize that the choice of a guitar as an accompanying instrument rules out such a hymn, as it does W. W. How's "For All the Saints" (SINE NOMINE tune by Ralph Vaughan Williams). During the nine years I pastored, there was a brief season of six to nine months when we sang without accompaniment because the building in which we met limited our accompanying instruments to those that limited hymn selection. We sang a better range of good worship music without accompaniment than we could have sung with it.

This chapter has mentioned just a few examples of the kinds of musical questions we would raise; many others could be raised. In each case, the question is this: if we are to accompany our lyrics with music, will the musical choices enhance or impede the congregation's expression of those lyrics? A primary musical concern with contemporary worship music is instrumentation: the guitar is usually selected as the accompanying instrument, which is ordinarily a poor instrument for accompanying chorus. But there are other musical concerns also: uninteresting rhythms, overwhelming percussion, predictable melodies, needless repetition, and so on. Further, the choice of worship music is limited to recently written songs, permitting us only a small amount of the church's overall repertoire—and not an especially good one at that.

Questions for Reflection

1. Are some rhythms more singable and accessible to a congregation than others? Can you think of an example?
2. What is timbre, and is it a significant musical component? Is a piece of music different if played on a flute than if played on a saxophone or trombone? If so, how?
3. Is harmony an important component to music? How do some instrumental accompaniments make harmony easier or more difficult?
4. Does the timbre of the guitar suit it well to accompany a chorus of voices? Is the guitar commonly used outside worship settings to accompany choruses? Why or why not? Does the use of the guitar to accompany congregational singing limit what songs can be sung? If so, how?

8

CONTEMPORANEITY
AS A VALUE

CONTEMPORANEITY IS A VALUE, or a value system, that prefers what is new to what is old. Contemporaneity views the past as passé, and tends to regard it either with benign disinterest or with outright contempt. Contemporaneity has several sources in our culture.[1]

The Cultural Sources of Contemporaneity

Technological Causes

Technological change contributes to contemporaneity by making generations without certain technologies appear

1. *Contemporaneity* is a rarely used word. I believe this is because our culture is so contemporaneous that we don't even notice it. Similarly, when Ken Myers describes pop culture as *banal*, he employs a word rarely used today. Our culture is so banal that we don't even notice it. *Paedocentric* is rarely employed in our culture because the entire culture *is* paedocentric. The reason is the same in each case: when a given value is all but universal in a culture, we come not to notice it as a choice or option (just as trout probably don't know they are wet). If this pattern persists, one could study cultures by the terms in their language that they do *not* use. These terms would tell us about values so omnipresent that the culture does not even notice them.

primitive. Since technological innovation now occurs at a faster pace than ever before, the natural cultural by-product is contemporaneity. Particular technologies claim to "revolutionize" human society, or some aspect of society, with the inevitable implication that society needed to have been revolutionized. We cannot exalt and declare the wonders of such new technologies without simultaneously declaring the superiority of cultures that have them compared to cultures that do not.

Technological change affects the current discussion in another, albeit subtler, way. Rapid change itself is profoundly significant to our human sensibilities. Rapid rates of change of any sort require us to adjust to change. And once we find ourselves adjusted to change, we adjust to its presence, and regard it either as a positive or at least as a neutral reality. In any period of rapid change, change becomes an acceptable reality: "It's the wave of the future." "You can't resist progress."

But this common sensibility that change is either uniformly positive or neutral may very well be mistaken. Not all change is good change. Germany certainly changed when Adolf Hitler assumed office; not every observer would call this change good. Similarly, the Soviet Union changed profoundly under Joseph Stalin, but then again the cost of that change was literally millions of Soviet deaths. The United States changed after the *Roe v. Wade* decision, but not all consider the change to have been good for us. In Henry F. Lyte's evensong referred to in the introduction to this volume, part of the second verse says: "change and decay in all around I see; O thou who changest not, abide with me." In Lyte's opinion, some change is associated with mortality and decay; God is appealed to as an unchanging Reality in the presence of vicissitude. But when a culture changes so rapidly that we do not have time to assess those changes, many simply adjust to change as an inevitable, if not a positive good. In such a culture, if the fundamental character of Christian worship changes profoundly in a decade or two, without any serious theological reflection, this is not a cause for concern. But for those who believe the Christian tradition *is* a tradition—a handing down of something previously experienced and regarded as precious—rapid change without significant theological defense is a cause for significant concern.

In addition to these two ways in which technological change cultivates contemporaneity, there are specific questions as well. Specifically, image-based technologies distance us from the past. When reading letters written by Civil War soldiers to relatives, for instance, we have a sense of communion with them. Language brings the past close to us, and it facilitates our sense of human similarity to others. But images do just the opposite; an old, grainy, sepia-toned photograph of a Civil War soldier makes him appear very distant. Indeed, a photograph of John Travolta dressed in a disco outfit from the 1970s makes him look ludicrously passé, even though he is still living (though with considerable and merited embarrassment about *Saturday Night Fever*). Since we are surrounded by images in our culture, we inevitably become contemporaneists.

Commercial Origins

Commerce, in its present American sense, would utterly fail, experiencing a financial crisis worse than that of 1929 (or

2009?), if the culture did not embrace the premise on which it is largely based: that what is newer is more valuable than what is older. One of the first commercials I recall seeing as a child was for Tide detergent, and I recall that in the late 1950s, Tide was advertised as "new and improved." Fifty years later, it is still advertised as "new and improved." It may well be improved (though I don't know how much detergent can be improved; after fifty-plus years of continued improvement, Tide should make coffee for me in the morning by now), but it certainly isn't "new." Yet "new" is the currency employed by Madison Avenue to sell almost everything. Commerce requires consumers to consume; and commerce manipulates consumption by creating a false sense of dissatisfaction with the old, so that individuals long for something newer.

Since commerce is such a large part of our culture, its messages implicitly praising newness bombard us frequently and persistently. Few people are wary enough to fend off this onslaught, and therefore most people become convinced that what is newer is better, even though there is little evidence to substantiate the claim. The new photocopier in our academic building will not do things that the old copier did easily. Technologically, it is superior because it is a "smart" copier that discerns the orientation of the words on a page; but practically, it is inferior because it automatically adjusts the image to this orientation, which makes it impossible to photocopy the two pages of an open book side-by-side. It is a technological marvel, but it won't do what photocopiers would easily do thirty years ago. It is newer, and surely more expensive; it is *not* better for my purposes. By contrast, the wedding vows from the old Anglican Book of Common

Prayer are still employed in many weddings, not because they are new, but because they are good.

For self-interested purposes, commercial forces "sell" the idea of contemporaneity in order to then sell whatever else it is they desire to sell. We expect no less of them. But we need not follow, lemming-like, their sales pitches for contemporaneity. I shave with a 1906 Gillette model double-edge safety razor. It is no longer manufactured by Gillette[2] because its replacement blades are very inexpensive, and the handle itself is comparatively inexpensive. Gillette can make much more money by selling expensive triple- or quadruple-blade razor cartridges, so it no longer has a commercial interest in the earlier model. But the earlier model shaves just as well (arguably better, though it requires a little skill), costs substantially less,[3] and doesn't fill landfills with plastic cartridges that take many years to decompose. By any ordinary definition, taking into consideration function, cost, and ecology, the 1906 model is vastly superior to the 2009 model; but Gillette has a significant commercial interest in selling the 2009 model. Gillette no longer manufactures the older model because it would prefer that consumers not know of the "competition." And probably more than 90 percent of the consumer market will take for granted the maxim that "newer is better," and will never even try the older model, nor know that over a lifetime, the individual consumer would save

2. It is manufactured in Solingen, Germany, a city that has a reputation for manufacturing some of the world's finest cutlery.

3. One of the better double-edge razor blades is the Feather DE, which costs about 50¢ each, so if they last for two weeks each, the annual cost is $13. The latest Gillette Fusion replacement cartridge costs $3 each, for an annual cost of $78. And even if the gross amount is not much ($65 difference), why pay six times as much?

hundreds of dollars (while reducing landfill waste) by using the older model.

Part of the proof that "newer" is the currency employed by commercial forces is that many of them now use even the future (*tomorrow's* "present") to sell their products. As an academic, for instance, I am frequently exposed to pamphlets, seminars, or "special" presentations about some product or another that is touted as "The Future of Education," as one mechanical messiah after another is paraded before a dubious faculty on the *ostensible* ground that it will make our students more learned, but on the *actual* (albeit unstated) ground that it will make the manufacturer more wealthy.

Not one of these ingenious gewgaws addresses the fundamental reality that many educators since Socrates have recognized: namely, that the barrier to education is the student *himself*—his parochialism, his laziness, his reluctance to abandon his current viewpoints, his resistance to disciplined intellectual effort, his complacent self-satisfaction with his present attainment and understanding. Nearly every capable educator in the history of the human race has realized that the least important thing we educators do is disseminate information, which is (especially now) widely available in less expensive formats. What capable educators have always attempted to do is to infect their students with a *love* of learning and a *hatred* of parochialism.[4]

4. This is the thesis behind Ezra Pound's famous aphorism: "Real education must ultimately be limited to men who insist on knowing, the rest is mere sheep-herding." *ABC of Reading* (New York: New Directions Publishing, 1960), 84. Similarly, Dr. Samuel Johnson said: "Curiosity is one of the permanent and certain characteristics of a vigorous intellect." *Rambler* no. 103 (March 12, 1751). The "unexamined life" that Socrates deplored in his day is equally deplorable (and perhaps even more common) in ours (Plato, *Apology of Socrates*, 38a).

The goal of every good educator is, and always has been, for our students to rediscover what they all knew intuitively as young children: the innocent and thrilling joy of discovery and understanding (a joy ordinarily crushed by compulsory education). At best, tools can assist those who already possess this love of learning, but no inanimate tool can or ever will infect a human with such love.

But education is big business (and perhaps even bigger politics) in our nation, and savvy commercial forces understandably wish to get their foot inside the academic door as far as they can.[5] So they continually manufacture two things in the effort to win the academic market: some new gizmo, and the *idea* that this gizmo is the "wave of the educational future" (without which the first would not be purchased). Obviously, if commercial forces can first create in us a desire to arrive at the future today, they can sell "tomorrow's" product to us on that ground. Such a point of view is merely contemporaneity in its most exaggerated form.

Media Origins: "The News"

Closely related to the discussion of commercial origins of contemporaneity is the particular commercial product that we ordinarily call "the news." We are so surrounded by news media that we hardly notice them; indeed, when many people talk about "the media," what they *mean* is "the news media." A

---

5. I say *understandably* because the purpose of any business is to make money. How much potential profit is there in putting chalkboards (which last many years) and chalk in every classroom? By comparison, how much potential profit is there in putting computers and computer projectors and screens (most of which last only a few years, and therefore must be replaced fairly frequently) in every classroom? To raise the question is to answer it.

medium, by definition, is merely a tool of communication, and communication media include orality (talking orally), handwriting, the printing press, radio, television, the Internet, and so forth. But since many of the most pervasive uses of media in our culture are devoted to producing news, many people equate "the media" and "the news media."

The news was not always so ubiquitous. In the late eighteenth century, many newspapers were published only twice monthly, on the perfectly sensible ground that important events, worthy of the public's attention, do not ordinarily happen with greater frequency than this. But when it became profitable to sell newspapers, some smart accountant realized that profits could be doubled by producing weekly newspapers. In time, some equally smart accountant realized that daily newspapers would provide even more revenue. And the race to produce news has not slowed since.

News is a commercial product. Provided that the product can be sold, there is always greater profit to be made in greater production. So news has become a commercial product: something that is manufactured, marketed, and sold. Part of that marketing, of course, relies on persuading people that it is important for them to know what has recently happened, an idea that has not been universally recognized as self-evident. In the early 1920s, Walter Lippmann wrote *Public Opinion*,[6] in which he expressed concern about whether the American Republic was well served if either governmental or commercial forces determined what information would inform the public. Having served as a propagandist during World War I,

6. New York: Harcourt, Brace and Co., 1922.

in which Lippmann and his Allied colleagues collaborated on which casualty figures to release (they always chose the lowest estimates for Allied losses and the highest for Germany's losses), Lippmann knew that public behavior corresponded not to reality (the actual environment in which we live), but to *reported* reality (which he called a "pseudo-environment"), which is not always the same.

Lippmann's line of reasoning and concern was articulated forty years later by Daniel J. Boorstin (who would later become Librarian of Congress) in *The Image: A Guide to Pseudo-Events in America.*[7] Boorstin, even more than Lippmann, commented on the commercial necessity of producing or manufacturing news, and he called attention to the invention of the "celebrity," an individual who is celebrated not for doing anything particularly noteworthy, but merely for being celebrated. Such people, Boorstin argued, are not worthy of the public's attention, but are created or manufactured by those who need more news. After all, genuinely significant individuals, whose actions might be worthy of the public's attention, just don't come along frequently enough to satisfy the demands of commerce, so we invent another category of people whose actions we call the public's attention to.

This Lippmann-Boorstin discussion reached a fairly current moment with the 1999 appearance of Professor C. John Sommerville's *How the News Makes Us Dumb: The Death of Wisdom in an Information Age.*[8] A historian, Sommerville has a predictable thesis: there is wisdom to be gained from giving our attention to things that happened some time ago (say, thirty years or more).

7. New York: Harper & Row, 1961.
8. Downers Grove, IL: InterVarsity Press, 1999.

The consequences of such events can be observed, and a chorus of interpreters of those consequences can place their thoughts before the public, which can judge whether the interpreters of those consequences are right, and whether lessons can be learned. But this cannot be done with what happened yesterday. We do not and cannot know the consequences of a recent event, nor is there time for competent interpreters to develop their interpretations. The news "makes us dumb" because we give our attention to what can never make us wiser.

Sommerville joined his voice to those of Lippmann and Boorstin in reminding us that commercial forces, and commercial forces alone, have cultivated the appetite for "the news." There is no other way to account for it, since there is no other reason to give attention to whatever has happened, simply because it *has* happened, and happened recently. But in giving so much attention to what is recent, Sommerville argues, we become contemporaneists, people who intuitively believe that giving attention to what is recent is more important than giving attention to what is not recent. Otherwise, why would I care to read a newspaper account of someone robbing a convenience store yesterday rather than read an account of Abraham Lincoln's presidency?[9] And again, it is entirely understandable that commercial forces will benefit from this; the question is why

9. Among some headlines I've noted recently from reputable news sources are these: "Bubba the Lobster Dies"; "Small Cars Fare Worse in Crash Tests"; "Polar Bear Mauls Woman at Berlin Zoo"; "Woody Harrelson Claims He Mistook Photographer for Zombie." Is it even remotely possible that giving our attention to such items would make us wiser or better citizens? Yet stories such as these prove that truly significant events, those worthy of a responsible public's attention, do not happen frequently, and that therefore other stories are placed before the public's attention—not because they are worthy of our attention, but because commercial forces wish to attract our attention to their commercial messages that are part of "the news."

we permit those commercial interests to dictate our choices and our values.

Notice that our vocabulary contains the expression "the news" and not the expression "the olds," though both concepts exist. Some events are recent; some events are not—but we have an expression for only the one, because only the one can be mass-produced and mass-marketed in a commercially viable way. But one cannot sell "the news" until one first sells the idea that "the new" is more important than "the old." Many events hold our attention merely because they are recent, proved by the fact that we almost never read a newspaper that is a week old. If a historian wrote a book about the mundane realities that appear in the newspaper (or on the televised news), no one would read the book. We expect historians to exercise good judgment about which events are *worthy* of our attention—an expectation with which we do not encumber "the news."

The reason *The Boston Globe* cannot sell me a newspaper is the same reason *Time* cannot sell me a weekly newsmagazine, which is the same reason I've never seen Katie Couric anchor the evening news: I don't believe recently occurring events are ordinarily worthy of my attention. And on the rare occasion when one is (September 11, 2001), enough people will be talking about it that I need not spend money or time to learn about it. Further, I am very self-aware of a value issue here: is something worthy of my (limited) attention merely because it occurred recently?

Philosophical Origins

Americans don't tend to read much philosophy. Therefore, insofar as philosophy influences us, it is probably only at an implicit level at best.[10] The following three philosophical movements, therefore, may have contributed to the easy acceptance of contemporaneity, but I would not wish to claim anything other than an indirect relationship.

Marxism. Karl Marx, following Georg Hegel, understood that the present historical moment is the inevitable emergence in the present out of the struggles and antitheses of the past. He argued not merely that revolution, pitting bourgeois and proletariat, was lawful or likely, but also that it was inevitable. Every historical moment is the emergence of a synthesis of the theses and antitheses of the past. Such a view of history implies that change is the norm (contrasted with theories of human history viewing change as abnormal). A static state is either illusory or brief, for Marx; the ordinary state is change. And once we grant that change is inevitable, there is a tendency to believe that it is right, normal, or good. Insofar as Marxist/ Hegelian ideas have percolated into our culture (and again, I care to make no guess about the degree of this), those ideas would probably contribute to contemporaneity: our moment is the inevitable and normal result of previous moments.

Progressivism. Progressivism, in its own way, suggests that human history is inexorably moving forward. Progressivism does not require a Hegelian substructure; it can (and probably does) ground itself as much on evolutionary ideas. But progressivism views change as both inevitable and good. As an intellectual

10. Some of the debate about Allan Bloom's *The Closing of the American Mind* (New York: Simon and Schuster, 1987), for instance, centered on the cogency of the claim that Friedrich Nietzsche had influenced our culture as pervasively as Bloom suggested.

posture, progressivism tends to view the present as the result of selfish and self-serving activities in the past, and therefore tends to wish to move toward the future as quickly as possible. In a technical sense, then, progressivism is *not* contemporaneous, because it wants the present to change. But it shares with contemporaneity contempt for the past.[11]

Since the American Republic is fairly young, compared to the Europe from which its original colonists arrived, it has comparatively little history. And since its colonists left the Old World for the New, they obviously distanced themselves from that past, and endeavored to create a *Novum Ordum Seclorum*. Americans have tended, therefore, to be forward-looking rather than past-looking, and thus tend to accept Henry Ford's dictum that "history is bunk." In a nontechnical and perhaps only implicit way, then, Americans have tended to be progressivists; as such, they regard the past with contempt, as do Marxists.

Historicism. A movement called *historicism* began originally in Germany in the early to mid-nineteenth century. Whereas *history* had previously been the study of the past, *historicism* was a methodological commitment to the idea that all things, to be properly explained, must be understood historically, in terms of the events and processes that caused them to come to be. As Maurice Mandelbaum put it, "Historicism is the belief that an adequate understanding of the nature of anything and an

---

11. Cf. the critique by Christopher Lasch, *The True and Only Heaven: Progress and Its Critics* (New York: Norton, 1991). For an alternative study of the opposite movement, consult Arthur Herman's *The Idea of Decline in Western History* (New York: Free Press, 1997).

adequate assessment of its value are to be gained by considering it in terms of the place it occupied and the role it played within a process of development."[12]

One would think that a movement so committed to a historical and contextual understanding of things would enhance and increase our respect for the past, but as historicism developed, it took an oddly different turn. A century earlier, many people believed that the past was hardly different from the present. David Hume may have been an example of this tendency:

> It is universally acknowledged that there is a great uniformity among the actions of men, in all nations and ages, and that human nature remains still the same.... Would you know the sentiments, inclinations, and course of life of the Greeks and Romans? Study well the temper and actions of the French and English.... Mankind are so much the same, in all times and places, that history informs us of nothing new or strange in this particular.[13]

But Hume's was not the only voice. Over two centuries earlier, the Renaissance and Reformation had "discovered" history—or, more precisely, had discovered anachronism, the idea that things might once have been substantially different than they are now (a matter that is obvious to us now). Indeed, the Reformation proceeded on precisely this particular anachronistic assumption: the present medieval church is different from the apostolic and ancient church, and we must reform

12. Maurice Mandelbaum, "Historicism," in *Encyclopedia of Philosophy* (New York: Macmillan, 1967, vol. 3), 24.

13. David Hume, "An Enquiry Concerning Human Understanding," in *The Harvard Classics*, ed. Charles W. Eliot, vol. 37 (New York: Collier & Son, 1938), 353–54.

the present medieval church in terms of its former, apostolic model. E. Harris Harbison understood the Reformation in precisely such terms:

> And to think more and more as historians and less and less as philosophers was to raise a disturbingly new question for Christian thinkers: What if there had been a breach of historical continuity within Christianity itself, a breach between a primitive apostolic Church close to its Founder's spirit and a corrupted institution of a later and darker age which had unwittingly broken the tie that bound it to Christ? What if the new history, archaeology, and philology should appear to shake to its foundations the structure of Christianity as a set of timeless beliefs?[14]

The Renaissance and Reformation, then, raised the possibility that the past may have been *different* from the present, and that the past could therefore provide important *perspective* for critically evaluating the present.

As historicism developed as a movement, the past was regarded as increasingly inaccessible to us. We do not "have" the past; we have *records* about the past, and those records can neither influence nor oblige us as the events themselves influenced or obliged those who were present. This idea was famously articulated by Gotthold Ephraim Lessing:

> That the Christ, against whose resurrection I can raise no important historical objection, therefore declared himself to be the Son of God; that his disciples therefore believed

14. E. Harris Harbison, *The Christian Scholar in the Age of the Reformation* (New York: Scribners, 1956), 35–36.

him to be such; this I gladly believe from my heart. For these truths, *as truths of one and the same class*, follow quite naturally on one another. But to jump with that historical truth to *a quite different class of truths* [italics mine], and to demand of me that I should form all my metaphysical and moral ideas accordingly: That, then, is the ugly, broad ditch which I cannot get across, however often and however earnestly I have tried to make the leap.[15]

For Lessing, there is now an "ugly, broad ditch" between himself and history, which he "cannot get across." History, as a mere record of what others observed, may interest me or even edify me, but it cannot *oblige* me or inform me about *reality*. Ironically, then, historicism ended up championing the idea of "the past-ness of the past," which is not at all what the term *historicism* would have communicated to most of us. At any rate, ironic or otherwise, historicism joined Marxism and progressivism in placing a barrier ("ugly, broad ditch") between us and the past. The past may amuse or interest us, but it cannot, said Lessing, *oblige* us. And if it cannot oblige us, it is largely irrelevant to us.

Whether or to what degree Marxism, progressivism, and historicism have influenced our culture is beyond my competence to judge, or my desire to assert. But each has had a similar tendency to regard the past with benevolent (or, in Marx's case, contemptuous) disregard. That is, when people such as Henry Ford dismissed history as "bunk," this may appear to have been little more than a hip-shot reflection;

15. *Lessing's Theological Writings*, ed. and trans. Henry Chadwick (Stanford, CA: Stanford University Press, 1956), 55.

and in Ford's case it may have been. But very serious thinkers had also argued the case quite energetically for well over a century before Ford. While the Reformation thought it could still build a bridge *to* the past, and learn *from* the past how to reform the present, by the time even of Lessing in the late eighteenth century, this "ditch" was judged to be uncrossable, as it is for so many today.

The Cultural Effect of Contemporaneity

The effect of contemporaneity is this: anything not contemporary seems odd, quaint, antiquated, outdated, or foreign. Its effect is to regard the past with a kind of benign contempt—benign because we know they meant well, but contempt because we don't seriously think that we could bring the values, traditions, or practices of the past into our moment. That is, we don't debate the past, we don't argue with it, and we don't even say that it was erroneous; we simply dismiss the past as passé.

Proponents of contemporary worship music, for instance, don't assert that the older hymn-writers wrote bad hymns (though some atrocious old hymns were indeed written), hymns that were theologically, literarily, or musically defective or perverse. They don't debate Paul Gerhardt's *theology* (the way many Calvinists debated the theology of some of Charles Wesley's or Fanny Crosby's hymns); they just dismiss his hymns as good hymns "for their time," and therefore *necessarily* unsuited to ours. A contemporaneist would no more sing Paul Gerhardt's hymns than dress in his seventeenth-century German garb.

The Cultural Value of Traditional

Those of us reared in the sixties recall that ours was a self-consciously "anti-traditional" subculture. That subculture, in large measure, produced the current culture, which is just as anti-traditional, but much less aware that it is so. That is, the sixties *knew* they were opposed to the antecedent culture and, ordinarily, for specific reasons: its conformity, its superficiality, its consumerism, its militarism, and so on. A contemporaneous culture, however, does not necessarily disagree with the past; it simply regards it as unworthy of attention. A contemporaneous culture desires to be hip, with it, and where it's at, and considers *traditional* to be equivalent to *parochial* or *complacent*.

But are such considerations neutral? Do they not reflect values, and if they do, are they consistent with Christianity? Are *tradition* and *traditional* connotatively bad words in Scripture? Jesus spoke negatively about "the tradition of the elders" when it contradicted divine teaching, and he had similar things to say about "your tradition" or "the tradition of men" (Matt. 15:2, 6; Mark 7:8, 9, 13). Paul also warned about the danger of "human tradition" that was contrary to God's (Col. 2:8). But neither said anything negative about tradition per se; they criticized human traditions only when they competed with divine instruction.

The New Testament also recognizes *good* traditions, traditions handed down from one generation to another that actually embody what is good. Paul doesn't praise the Corinthians for much, but he does "commend" them for maintaining "the traditions even as I delivered them to you" (1 Cor. 11:2). And Paul commanded the Thessalonians to "stand firm and hold to the traditions that you were taught by us, either by our spoken word or by our letter" (2 Thess. 2:15; cf. also 3:6).

Lexically, all that the Greek verb or noun means is "to hand over"; a tradition is something that one party hands over to another. Indeed, the most common use of the verb in the New Testament is for the "handing over" of the Son of Man to be crucified; the verb is often translated "betray," and Judas Iscariot himself is known by the term "the betrayer/the hander-over-er." But it is also used to describe the apostolic tradition, the things the apostles "handed over" or "delivered" to the other saints.

> For I received from the Lord what I also *delivered* to you, that the Lord Jesus on the night when he was betrayed took bread. (I Cor. 11:23)

> For I *delivered* to you as of first importance what I also received: that Christ died for our sins in accordance with the Scriptures. (I Cor. 15:3)

> Beloved, although I was very eager to write to you about our common salvation, I found it necessary to write appealing to you to contend for the faith that was once for all *delivered* to the saints. (Jude 3)

Thus, the Scriptures do not view tradition negatively; they assume that cultures, families, and individuals will "hand over" or "deliver" ideas, values, and customs to one another, and the question is merely whether a *specific* tradition is a good thing or a bad thing. But insofar as it would be virtually impossible for anyone to learn or experience Christianity apart from a tradition, tradition is a good thing. The Christian faith is handed on from one generation to another, as a very good thing. John Murray, in his excellent article "Tradition: Romish and Protestant," said this:

> For example, a reformed community breathes in a certain atmosphere, is animated by a certain spirit, embraces a certain viewpoint, is characterized by a certain type of life and practice, maintains and promotes certain types of institutions. We call this the reformed tradition; it permeates the whole life of that community. When we pass on to another community of a different tradition, we immediately notice the difference. In these respects the fact of tradition and of its all-permeating influence on thought and life is undeniable. Where it is a good tradition, it should be welcomed, embraced, cherished, promoted. It is the way whereby God in His providence and grace establishes and furthers His kingdom in the world.[16]

Anti-traditionalism per se—the rejection of all contact with the previous experience of Christianity—is therefore not Christian, and is certainly incompatible with the Apostles' Creed.[17] A disregard not only for the scriptural

16. *Collected Writings of John Murray*, vol. 4, *Studies in Theology* (Edinburgh: Banner of Truth Trust, 1982), 264–73.

17. I recognize that I am saying, in some sense, that the so-called free-church movement is un-Christian or sub-Christian. I believe it is sub-Christian or imperfectly Christian, and therefore, in some respects, un-Christian. To refuse to confess creedally some beliefs about God, or to refuse to join the rest of the catholic church in so doing, is, effectively, to deny the church catholic. And those of us who weekly confess to believe in the church catholic must recognize that we thereby disagree with those who reject it. I even consider the expression *free-church tradition* to be oxymoronic, since the so-called free church does not receive what has been handed down from previous generations and since it refuses to hand down anything to subsequent generations. The free-church movement (I prefer to call it a *movement*) is therefore halfway toward being a cult. Cults are ordinarily defined by two criteria: they reject the church catholic (and therefore recognize no sacraments

tradition itself, but for those from whom we have received it is contrary to Paul's injunction to Timothy:

> But as for you, continue in what you have learned and have firmly believed, *knowing from whom you learned it and how from childhood* you have been acquainted with the sacred writings, which are able to make you wise for salvation through faith in Christ Jesus. (2 Tim. 3:14–15)

Therefore, while it is not un-Christian to reject a *particular* traditional hymn, if it fails to satisfy appropriate theological, literary, or musical criteria, it is un-Christian to reject out of hand all connection to the rest of the catholic church, as though their prayers, examples, faith, hope, or, yes, hymns could not possibly be expected to assist us.

Further, if contemporaneity is inconsistent with Christianity, if its dismissal of the past is inconsistent with what the Scriptures teach, then the question sharpens: not only is it not *necessary* or *preferable* for worship song to sound contemporary, it is a positive *liability*. That is, if a song sounds contemporary, it already has one strike against it, and needs to overcome that strike by being extraordinarily good in every other way. If the meta-message of a contemporary-sounding hymn discourages our memory of those who have preceded us, and discourages an appreciation for their faith, witness, or gifts, then the rest of that hymn faces an uphill climb. It must excel in the other criteria to overcome this liability.

---

but their own as valid), and they reject some other point of orthodoxy in the Apostles' or Nicene Creed (ordinarily a Christological point). The free-church movement does not reject any particular part of the Apostles' or Nicene Creed, but does effectively deny the church catholic. We should, I suggest, return the favor.

By analogy, suppose the piano used to accompany hymn-singing at church were out of tune. Would it be lawful to use it? Of course. Would it be better to use it than to have no accompaniment at all? Probably so. But it would be an impediment or, at best, a mixed blessing. Similarly, when we sing praise to an everlasting God, or sing about a Redeemer who died for us over two millennia ago, but do so employing musical forms that imply that the past is passé, we are communicating a mixed message. If a contemporary-sounding hymn is otherwise excellent, then I think we can survive it, especially in small doses. But again, it would need to excel in the other criteria in order to compensate for its defect here.

Therefore, if a given church believes that it must use the occasional contemporary-sounding idiom of music, it should at least be as discreet about the matter as it possibly can. Accompany it, for instance, with something other than a guitar, so that the ubiquitous musical instrument of our moment does not add to the contemporaneous meta-message. And surely, surely, no well-thinking church that employed such forms would *advertise* that it was doing so. Bad enough to do it on occasion; even worse to call attention to the doing of it. Imagine a sign outside a church that read: "Piano out of tune: Come sing with us!" Well, if we must use an out-of-tune piano, let us do so as best we can; but let us not advertise the liability.

I am not unaware that the psalms say, "Oh sing to the LORD a new song" (Ps. 96:1). Indeed, the expression "new song" appears six times in the Psalter, always favorably (33:3; 40:3; 98:1; 144:9; 149:1). It also appears three other times in the Scriptures (Isa. 42:10; Rev. 5:9; 14:3). Nine times the Scriptures either urge us to sing a new song or at least approve of it when others do so. But this cannot be appropriately employed as an argument for singing contemporary-sounding songs, for the following reasons.

First, the adjective *old* appears as a general term of approval more frequently in the psalms than does the adjective *new*.[18] God, for instance, is affirmed to have been "enthroned from of old" (Ps. 55:19; cf. also 74:12; 77:11; 93:2), just as his mercy and steadfast love are celebrated as having been from of old (Ps. 25:6; cf. 74:12; 89:19, 49). In fact, I count thirteen approving uses of the adjective *old* in the psalms, and only seven approving uses of *new*. The psalms, that is, are not *contemporaneous*, in the value-establishing sense in which I have been using the word.

Second, a "new song" is not the same as a "song that sounds new." The hymns that James Boice and Paul Jones wrote in the last year of Dr. Boice's life are "new," but they do not necessarily *sound* new.[19] Biblically, the "new song" in each circumstance is due to some new act of deliverance on God's part, and the people are urged to celebrate with new songs, songs suited to commemorating the new deed. If God were to do such an act of public deliverance of his people today, for instance, I would not object at all to a song being composed for the occasion. But the Scriptures do not say that the song composed for that occasion should sound new.[20]

18. Though the expression "old song" does not appear in Scripture.

19. James Montgomery Boice and Paul Steven Jones, *Hymns for a Modern Reformation* (Philadelphia: Tenth Presbyterian Church, 2000).

20. From what little we know of the musical practices of ancient Israel, her canting/chanting of the psalms was virtually unchanged from her earliest days to her last days. That is, insofar as we understand her Psalter practices (and we really do not know as much as we would like), the evidence suggests that none of her "new songs" sounded new; they were, in their formal properties, indistinguishable from the ancient songs.

Third, in plain point of fact, the vast majority of the biblical psalms were old at any given moment, and the Israelites plainly sang them. They continued to sing, for instance, Psalm 90 after their return from Babylonian captivity, even though that psalm is attributed to Moses (its superscription, part of the original Hebrew manuscript, reads, "A Prayer of Moses, the Man of God"). Psalms 78, 106, and 137, for instance, all celebrate God's delivering his people from captivity. But these three psalms did not, after the exile, replace the other 147 psalms, which Israel continued to sing.

Fourth, although I do not profess to be familiar with every contemporary song or chorus out there, I've never heard one that was a "new song" in this biblical sense, of being composed to celebrate some *recent* act of God's deliverance of his people. That is, if individuals or groups wish to draft the Psalter's commendation of "new song" into this discussion, then the rest of us have every right to ask them (charitably, of course) to do so honestly: to understand honestly what those passages are actually commending (songs commemorating God's acts of public deliverance), and to compose, honestly, songs that do so, rather than songs that merely "sound new," which the Scriptures nowhere require or approve.

At any moment in Israel's later history, the vast majority of the psalms she sang were very old—centuries old and sometimes more than a millennium old. If we seriously or honestly wished to suggest that our practices should follow those of biblical Israel after the return from captivity, we would insist that 90 percent of our songs today be more than a thousand years old, which I doubt anyone (including myself) would wish to do. There is no biblical proof text for singing songs that sound new *or* for songs that sound old. That question must be determined on other grounds, such as the grounds that I am suggesting in these chapters.

Questions for Reflection

1. As a review, what is *contemporaneity?*
2. What are some of the cultural sources and causes of contemporaneity's widespread prevalence in our culture?
3. Is all cultural change progress? Why or why not?
4. Is all technological change progress? Why or why not?
5. Do commercial interests promote contemporaneity; and if so, why?
6. While we call the gospel "good news," is it truly "new" anymore?
7. Walter Lippmann, Daniel Boorstin, and C. John Sommerville have all suggested that widespread consumption of "the news" is not healthy for cultures or individuals. Why did they think this?
8. Why isn't there an industry called "the olds"?
9. Do historians write about *anything* from the past, or what they judge to be the *significant* events of the past?
10. Did the Protestant Reformers look to the present, to the recent past, or to the distant past for instruction and guidance in reforming the church? Why?
11. Does the movement called "historicism" connect us *to* the past, or distance us *from* the past? How so?
12. Do the Holy Scriptures ever speak approvingly of tradition? If so, in what context?

13. Which adjective appears more frequently, in an approving sense, in the psalms: *old* or *new*? Why do you think this is?

14. Does the scriptural use of the expression "new song" justify discarding older songs? Why or why not? Does "new song" in the book of Psalms mean "a song that *sounds* new"? If not, what does it mean?

9

SONG AND PRAYER

IN THE SCRIPTURES, praying and singing praise are very closely related. Paul, for instance, told the Corinthians, "I will pray with my spirit, but I will pray with my mind also; I will sing praise with my spirit, but I will sing with my mind also" (I Cor. 14:15). Note that Paul regulates prayer and singing praise by the same considerations. Similarly, Psalm 90 is called "A Prayer of Moses," and indeed, in the Septuagint,[1] the ordinary New Testament word for *prayer* is used. Yet plainly it is a psalm, which was undoubtedly chanted in Israel. Routinely in the book of Psalms, the psalmist refers to his psalms as "prayers":

> Hear a just cause, O LORD; attend to my cry!
>> Give ear to my prayer from lips free of deceit! (Ps. 17:1)

> Hear my prayer, O LORD,
>> and give ear to my cry. (Ps. 39:12)

1. The Septuagint, or LXX, is the Greek translation of the Old Testament.

By day the LORD commands his steadfast love,
    and at night his *song* is with me,
    a *prayer* to the God of my life. (Ps. 42:8)

Apparently, then, many psalms or hymns are effectively prayers that are sung. Thus, some of the considerations by which we would evaluate prayers could and should also be considerations by which we could and should evaluate hymns (excepting those additional criteria germane only to music). That is, the fact that a prayer is sung rather than spoken is not a sufficient reason to alter the criteria by which we evaluate such a prayer. But would anyone seriously suggest, when evaluating prayers, that their evaluation is "just a matter of taste"? Do we not know, experientially, that some prayers are superior to other prayers in a number of ways? Are some prayers not more appropriate than others, more edifying? In the mid-nineteenth century, Samuel Miller taught a course on prayer at Princeton Seminary, and later compiled his notes in written form and published *Thoughts on Public Prayer*, totaling 306 pages. Miller devoted the fifth chapter to "Characteristics of a Good Public Prayer." Would not our songs in worship be rightly informed by the considerations regarding public prayer?

I have suggested to my students, for instance, that one of the tests of a hymn is whether it would exist as Christian verse if it were not put to music. Many do; we often find ourselves quoting portions of hymns to one another in conversation, when an especially apt religious reality has been well expressed by some hymn-writer. I can recall this happening to me in conversation several times in just the last two weeks.[2] Some of what we now know as William Cowper's hymns were in fact poetry for many years before they were put to music. In fact, if you leaf your way through *The Oxford Book of Christian Verse*, you will find not only Cowper, but many other poets/hymn-writers, indicating that many hymns were originally written as Christian verse by people who were published poets in their own right, who brought the same literary talent to their hymn-writing. Consider this partial list from that volume: George Herbert, Thomas Shepherd, Charles Wesley, William Wordsworth, Alfred, Lord Tennyson, John Henry Newman, Richard C. Trench, Augustus Toplady, Elizabeth Barrett Browning, Horatius Bonar, John Mason Neale, Robert Steven Hawker, John Milton, John Newton, Christina Georgina Rossetti, Richard W. Dixon, Philip Doddridge, John Donne, John Dryden, William Blake, George Crabbe.

This incomplete list of poets who wrote hymns is almost a *Who's Who* of English poetry. Hymn-writing, in other words, was high, serious art. These poems were not dashed off in half an hour, but were labored over with all the creativity of masterly poets. This poetry would have survived, indeed *has* survived, apart from musical settings. Not every hymn would satisfy this criterion, but should not every hymn at least aspire to satisfy it? Is not doggerel put to music still doggerel?

I fear that the cart may have gotten well before the horse. In some circles, as long as a chorus sounds contemporary, it

2. I might be stretching my middle-aged memory here, but I believe in just the last couple of weeks, I have had occasion to quote portions of "Abide with Me," "All Praise to God, Who Reigns Above," "How Sweet and Awesome Is the Place," and "A Mighty Fortress Is Our God."

is judged to be both acceptable and appropriate to the Christian assembly, without regard for the kinds of theological and literary criteria that make the psalms, for instance, so excellent. Totally apart from any musical considerations, both individuals and congregations routinely find the psalms to be edifying for use in private, family, or corporate worship. Would our typical contemporary worship music choruses, if the music were removed, edify in the way the psalms do? To raise the question is to answer it: very few would be acceptable to us if they were not accompanied by a guitar.[3] If our pastor's prayers were as inconsequential or meaningless as most of these songs are, we would find them to be unbearable.

Questions for Reflection

1. Does the apostle Paul regulate singing and praying by similar (or even identical) standards? Which standards?
2. Are many of the canonical psalms in fact "prayers"? Give an example.
3. Would or should the lyrics of a good hymn survive in the Christian tradition even if they were not set to music? Have any such hymn lyrics survived as poetry?

---

3. Exceptions would probably include some of the thoughtful lyrics of Stuart Townend, whose "In Christ Alone" and "How Deep the Father's Love" would, in my estimation, satisfy the ordinary standards of any hymnal revision committee. Townend and others like him prove that contemporary artists can add their best work to the church's hymnic canon. An artist such as Townend is not satisfied that his work sounds contemporary; it must also be *good*. Further, works such as these demonstrate that we may need to distinguish contemporary *hymns* from contemporary *praise choruses*. While both employ guitar, and while both make other musical choices that have the effect of making them sound new, other formal properties distinguish them.

10

THE MIND, SENTIMENT, AND SENTIMENTALITY

ONE OF PAUL'S many directives to the Corinthians was this:

> For if I pray in a tongue, my spirit prays but my mind is unfruitful. What am I to do? I will pray with my spirit, but I will pray with my mind also; I will sing praise with my spirit, but I will sing with my mind also. (1 Cor. 14:14–15)

For Paul, prayer and song should engage the mind, and for this reason must be lyrically intelligible, articulated in a known language. This introduces his even more general comment that worship must be intelligible to be edifying: "Otherwise, . . . how can anyone in the position of an outsider say 'Amen' to your thanksgiving when he does not know what you are saying?" (1 Cor. 14:16). Some people wish to bypass Paul's concern for intelligible worship, and go directly to emotional experience alone.

Sentiment ordinarily refers to those internal stirrings of human emotion or passion that are merited by that to which one is exposed. So the sense of awe that one experiences standing at the rim of the Grand Canyon is elicited by the actual grandeur the canyon possesses. The internal sentiment of being awestruck is thus merited by the external prompting. *Sentimentality*, on the other hand, designates the desire to experience that which is moving, even if there is no external occasion to prompt the feeling. In this sense, sentimentality is *un*merited or *un*justified emotional stirring or passion.

On occasion, individuals who are prone to sentimentality will read a biblical injunction about joy, for instance, and then assume that worship is inadequate unless a certain emotional experience occurs, as though the emotional stirring were itself valuable. I suggest, however, that unmerited feelings have no merit, almost tautologically. If the (external and objective) substance of a hymn, prayer, or sermon provokes appropriate emotional response, all well and good; but to manufacture such a response without a corresponding reason is just sentimentality: emotion for emotion's sake.

Music enters this sphere of conversation because some music has qualities that evoke emotional responses cheaply and quickly, without engaging the entire person, and especially without engaging the mind. Much of the debate during the time of Romantic music related to this question whether it was appropriate to appeal to passion without regard for certain formal, intellectual, structural properties in music. In our particular moment, one side of the debate has effectively carried the day because many people come to evaluate music by its property to stimulate their emotions without any corresponding objective

134

or formal ground. This may even be the primary quality that some people like in music. Such individuals tolerate, even enjoy and promote, worship music that has little in its lyrics to elicit appropriate or modulated emotion, as long as the music itself triggers an emotional rush of some sort.

Personally, I think this is a major reason that people tolerate contemporary worship music. Few of its lyrics would provoke any emotional response *if they were not set to music.*[1] By contrast, many of the lyrics of genuinely good hymns have provoked profound and appropriate religious sentiment when they existed as poetry before they were put to music (such as William Cowper's poems); and indeed, some of these still provoke religious sentiment even when not accompanied by music. "O Sacred Head, Now Wounded" works just about as well without music as it does with it, as does the eventide hymn "Abide with Me," though each has been set to particularly apt music.

Often, not only do we prefer sentimentalistic music to music that is not (music whose passion is more restrained, as Johannes Brahms's famously was), we also prefer music that promotes or provokes *happy* sentiments. We prefer music that is cheerful, that gives us an emotional lift. A student in my Psalms class found it interesting that about half the psalms (73 of 150) are laments, and that there are lament elements in some of the others. On his own time, he worked his way through the little praise-chorus book employed in our chapel at the college, and

---

1. To be fair, some musicians have recently responded to the earlier criticisms of contemporary worship music, and there is some evidence of improvement in the lyrics by some who are writing contemporary hymns, although the musical quality continues to suffer.

reported to me later that there was not a single lament in it. Mathematically, half of Israel's psalms were laments; none of my students' songs are. Now, perhaps some of Israel's laments were due to her distinct place in the history of redemption, longing for a Redeemer who had not yet appeared historically. And perhaps some were due to God's infliction of temporal judgments on her for her rebellion and idolatry. But many were due to her own sinfulness, her own unfaithfulness and guilt, and the shame they produced. Is there no place in the Christian assembly for similar realities? And though God's judgment for our sin has now fallen on Christ, rather than in the form of temporal punishments on our nation, is this *lesser* reason to lament or *greater* reason to lament?

> Who was the guilty who brought this upon thee?
> Alas, my treason, Jesus, hath undone thee.
> 'Twas I, Lord Jesus, I it was denied thee:
> I crucified thee.

> . . . .

> For me, kind Jesus, was thine incarnation,
> Thy mortal sorrow, and thy life's oblation:
> Thy death of anguish and thy bitter passion,
> For my salvation.[2]

2. Johann Heermann wrote the lyrics to "Ah, Holy Jesus" in 1630, inspired by a Latin hymn alternatively ascribed to Augustine or Jean de Fecamp (1000–1079), and within a decade Johann Crüger had written musical accompaniment (HERZLIEBSTER JESU) so apt that J. S. Bach employed it in part of his *St. Matthew Passion* in 1727. In 1899 Robert Bridges translated the lyrics for the benefit of the English-speaking world, much of which still employs Crüger's musical setting.

The lyrics of such a hymn stir our emotions, and they do so appropriately, as they focus our attention on the awful, awe-inducing reality of Christ's substitutionary death for us. Such lyrics draw cool, world-infected hearts into an appropriately warm consideration of what the Savior has done. But they are like Israel's laments in their pensive, sorrowful character. If a Christian hymnal (or chorus book) has no place for such texts of lament, it has no place for Christ himself.[3]

At least many Romanticist composers were aware of what they were doing, and of the choices they were making. Richard Wagner knew what he was doing in freeing music from what he judged to be the constraints of rational thought, even while he observed some of the same formal musical properties observed by Brahms, for instance. The Romantic theory believed that music could express the inexpressible, in some sense.[4] But it did not deny the importance of language (and hence rational thought) in other modes of communication, and the program music so characteristic of the Romantic era was more lyrical than the Classical music that preceded it. But in our day, our preference for mindless sentimentality is not the result of serious reflection or philosophical conviction; it is mainly the result of being surrounded by

3. It doesn't surprise me that a commercial artist such as Thomas Kinkade sells so many of his paintings to evangelical Christians. The same upbeat, sin-free (and therefore dying-Redeemer-free) sentimentality that characterizes Kinkade's paintings characterizes much of contemporary evangelical worship music. His paintings depict a world never fallen and therefore never redeemed by a Mediator's dying, whose joys and glory reside only in the creation, not in the Creator. Voltaire's *Candide* satirized the very worldview that Kinkade portrays and that evangelical Christians consume.

4. For a fairly nontechnical discussion, cf. the standard introduction by Donald Jay Grout, *A History of Western Music, Revised* (New York: Norton, 1973), esp. 537–46.

such sentimentality via the commercial airwaves. We hear so much music that is sentimentalistic that nothing else sounds like music to us; we say that we "prefer" such music when, in fact, we have not heard enough of the alternative for it to even register as music in our corporate psyche. And as I have suggested in many other places in this volume, not only have we consumed the products that commercial forces have sold us, but we have "bought" their values and sensibilities also.

In a culture whose various mediating institutions have encouraged sentimentality, it is not surprising that sentimentalistic music is the preferred, if not the only, music that some listen to. Some individuals may not have cultivated their sensibilities to the point that they can appreciate music that provokes sentiment but not sentimentality. They expect everything to be obvious, direct, "in your face," and are disappointed with art forms that do not provide this obvious emotional pop. But this expectation may merely prove that these people are fairly uncultivated or that our culture is comparatively barbaric—and there is no particular reason that the church should accommodate or encourage such unrefined sensibilities.

Questions for Reflection

1. Is it possible to distinguish between *sentiment* and *sentimentality*? If so, what makes them different? Are they equally appropriate in worship?

2. Does our culture prefer music that provokes happy sentiments or sad sentiments? Does it prefer to "feel good" or

"feel humbled"? Does Christianity endorse or promote unmixed happiness in this life?

3. Of the seven genres within the psalms, which is the largest genre, constituting almost half of the Psalter?

4. How, if at all, is the present discussion similar to the discussions during Romanticism's rise in music?

II

RITUAL (FORMALITY AND INFORMALITY)

PART OF WHAT DISTINGUISHES the traditional hymns of the church from contemporary worship music is that the one is fairly formal, whereas the other is fairly informal. Ours is, of course, an informal culture, and becoming more so all the time. As recently as 1960, public officials wore top hats to presidential inaugurations, and this is becoming less common. If you view a photograph of a baseball game around the time of the Second World War, you will observe that nearly all the men in the stands were wearing a hat (a fedora, not a baseball cap), a white shirt, and a tie. Plainly, this has all changed, and the rejection of ritual, a rejection so important to the sixties, has remained the standard of our culture. But nothing is neutral; every cultural change has potential deficits and credits, and we must give some thought to such a matter.

Cultural anthropologists have noted that every civilization has rituals of some sort, and that the sociological or cultural purpose of ritual is to invest an event with significance. Marriages, funerals, inaugurations, anniversaries, birthdays, and other rituals function to convey importance: to distinguish the special from the mundane. In distinguishing what is deemed significant, ritual tends to do three things to serve this end: ritual ensures that a matter will be remembered (anniversaries, memorials, national holidays); ritual celebrates achievement (commencement exercises, athletic awards dinners, Eagle Scout ceremonies); and ritual confers membership (immigration swearing-in ceremonies, initiation rites). Thus, as long as cultures or subcultures consider some things to be important, they will wish to remember and celebrate these important matters. The fact that ritual is on the decline in the United States today may prove the point that authors such as Ken Myers, David Denby, John McWhorter, and Todd Gitlin have made: that we have become trivial.

In this transitional phase, as we move in an increasingly trivial direction and therefore have fewer rituals (and the forms that attended them) than we once did, at the present moment we are somewhat inconsistent. We haven't rejected all ritual. It isn't uncommon for one of my students to show up at church in jeans and a T-shirt, and to stand in front of the church, playing a guitar. The same student, a year later, gets married. At his wedding, he and his groomsmen have rented tuxedos, and the bridesmaids are wearing formal (and expensive!) gowns. Why? Well, at an intuitive level, people regard their marriages as important and significant (and they are), and so they still expend considerable effort and money to ritualize the event with forms that confer significance.

This is all well and good, and I do not object to it. I merely raise the question whether one's wedding day is as significant as the first day of the week, on which Christ left the tomb, and therefore on which the Christian church has always assembled to celebrate our release from mortality. So when certain events and the rituals that attend them seem "stuffy" or "formal," there is a good reason for it. My daughter and her soccer team-mates all dressed up nicely for her high school soccer awards banquet; it was an appropriate way of celebrating their team and individual accomplishments. But, of course, some of the young ladies dressed more formally that night than they do for church—signifying, I suppose, that a soccer goal is more important than the death and resurrection of Christ. That is, I suppose I'm encouraging a fish-or-cut-bait choice here: either continue to dress up for weddings (and for funerals) as a means of investing such events with out-of-the-ordinary significance, and do the same for our meeting with the triune God on the day of the resurrection; or remove ritual and formality from *all* parts of life. But no one believes his or her wedding day is more important than Resurrection Day (which, by the way, occurs fifty-two times a year, not once).

What has happened is that the church has followed (rather than led) its trivial, ironic, and banal culture. It has adopted the forms of a culture that rarely regards human life to be significant, and that therefore dispenses with those sociological customs and rituals by which cultures invest certain events or achievements with significance. But the question is not whether this is our "natural" culture (it is today); the question is whether we wish to communicate that nothing in life deserves to be ritualized—

and more specifically whether we wish to communicate that meeting with God doesn't deserve ritual.

The sixties generation largely dispensed with ritual and formality because the existing forms of ritual and formality were those of the parent generation, against which the sixties rebelled. In doing so, the sixties indicated its philosophical indebtedness to Romanticism and primitivism (and, if Allan Bloom was right, nihilism). That is, behind the rowdy adolescent shrieking of the sixties were some fairly serious philosophical ideas, yet the ideas were not very compatible with Christian theism. For theism, human life itself is significant because we bear the image of God. The world we live in is significant because it is God's creation. And some of the things that we bearers of God's image do in God's creation are more important than others, and we invest these significant things with appropriate meaning through ritual and form.

Some religious and theological movements have also exacerbated the situation. German Pietism of the seventeenth century arrived in North America thinly disguised as what we call revivalism or evangelicalism. Originally, in Germany, Pietism was a reaction to and rejection of the state church. The state church was, in large measure, moribund, as I believe all state churches eventually become. The solution, in my judgment, is to remove any civil support for the church, and effectively thereby remove the equivalent of civil servants from the gospel ministry.[1] Students of Pietism weren't able to think this way, however. They thought the problems had other sources, and

---

1. Cf. Darryl Hart, *A Secular Faith: Why Christianity Favors the Separation of Church and State* (Chicago: Ivan Dee, 2006).

they developed four distinctive emphases, unwittingly borrowed from Romanticism:

- They preferred the subjective to the objective ("heart" to the "head," we would say).
- They preferred the spontaneous to the planned (rejecting the Lutheran liturgy).
- They emphasized the individual *I* more than the corporate *we*.
- They emphasized the small group (they called it the *collegia pietatis*) rather than the visible church as the source of spiritual growth.

Pietism was (and is) therefore a somewhat deliberately anti-formal approach to Christianity. When it blends with a culture that is also moving in anti-formal and anti-ritualistic ways, far from resisting the culture's movement, it accelerates it.

Regardless of its source, the result is the same: an unwitting and therefore unintended conveying either that nothing is genuinely significant or that the meeting between the ascended Christ and his people is not significant, either of which I judge to be seriously erroneous and seriously sub-Christian. We are still, as the psalmist, "fearfully and wonderfully made" (Ps. 139:14), and as bearers of God's image, we can be sure that our lives will never be insignificant. To the contrary, our lives, unlike those of animate beings that do not bear God's image, will always be significant, and some moments more so than others.[2] Those that we judge

---

2. Yesterday morning we took a stray cat, which we had been feeding for about a month, to the vet, extremely ill. The vet recommended euthanizing him, and did so.

to be more so we invest with forms or rituals that convey such significance.

Professor Leland Ryken of Wheaton College once observed: "Earlier in this century someone claimed that we work at our play and play at our work. Today the confusion has deepened: we worship our work, work at our play, and play at our worship."[3] His observation is truer now than when he first made it, as a new generation now witnesses a new oxymoron for the first time: playful worship. We cannot deformalize or deritualize worship without turning it into play. But once we have done so, once we have removed those forms and rituals that once conveyed significance on worship, it is not at all surprising that we employ less formal music in those meetings. If we are willing to tolerate "Worship Lite," we should have no objections to "Music Lite." The other side of the coin is equally true: if we employ "Music Lite," we will inevitably have "Worship Lite."

Questions for Reflection

1. Compared to fifty or sixty years ago, is American culture more formal or less formal? How can you tell?
2. What is the primary sociological role of ritual? What are some of the more specific roles of ritual?
3. Were the 1960s "pro-ritual" or "anti-ritual"?
4. Was Pietism "pro-ritual" or "anti-ritual"? What were some of Pietism's preferences and distinctives?

We were sorry for the little animal, that his life had not been healthier or longer; but we did not have a funeral for him because he did not bear God's image.

3. *Redeeming the Time: A Christian Approach to Work and Leisure* (Grand Rapids: Baker, 1995), 12.

5. Discuss Professor Leland Ryken's comment: "Earlier in this century someone claimed that we work at our play and play at our work. Today the confusion has deepened: we worship our work, work at our play, and play at our worship."

12

STRATEGIC ISSUES

I PREFACE THE DISCUSSION of strategic considerations with a reminder that it is my final consideration. Much of the confusion and disagreement on this matter is due to making this the first consideration, prior to the others, and thereby terminating most conversations in anger and confusion before the relevant issues are even discussed. Once an individual, for instance, is committed to the proposition that we must use contemporary forms to "reach" our culture, he is not likely to be able to entertain any of the other considerations open-mindedly.[1] His appropriate and noble interest in the church's mission causes

---

1. I am unaware of any contest for "worst expressions ever added to the church's vocabulary." If there were such a contest, however, my nomination would be this: *reaching people for Christ*. This ambiguous expression (which never appears in Scripture) is redolent with positive connotative content, while being surprisingly bereft of much denotative value (what does it *mean*, anyway?). Who could be opposed to reaching people for Christ? Yet what does *reach* mean? Does it mean any sort of contact that has any vestige of religious content? Driving on Route 128 north of Boston one day, I was startled when a car passed me on the left, then without signaling immediately swerved in front of me, requiring me to hit the brakes. This vehicle displayed a bumper sticker: "Honk if you love Jesus." Well, I did honk, and I do love Jesus, but I still wish he had "reached me for Christ" by another method than that of almost causing an accident.

him to regard with contempt those deemed less zealous than he to "reach" the lost. Similarly, an individual who perceives the adoption of contemporary forms as "selling out" to the culture, or capitulating to the culture, will find it difficult to entertain the other considerations thoughtfully and fairly.

So the relation between missional/strategic concerns, on the one hand, and the questions of integrity in worship, on the other, needs to be discussed clearly, lest we injure either concern in our pursuit of the other.[2] Each is a valid and important consideration, but the failure to think clearly about their intersection causes problems. One presupposition that informs the following comments is this: I do not believe that any strategic question is *merely* a strategic question. Strategic issues arise when we discuss preaching, for instance, but no discussion of preaching is *merely* a strategic discussion. To discuss preaching requires that we also consider exegetical questions, liturgical questions, and theological questions.

Meeting of Saints with God, or Evangelistic Meetings

Julius Melton, in his *Presbyterian Worship in America: Changing Patterns Since 1787*,[3] traced the effects of revivalism on religious traditions in America that had antedated revivalism.[4] In such communions (such as the Presbyterian), wor-

---

We can have many kinds of contact with people, but not all of those methods are even remotely likely to serve a genuinely useful spiritual or religious end.

2. Thoughtful consideration of both matters animated and informed Marva Dawn's helpful book, *Reaching Out without Dumbing Down: A Theology of Worship for These Urgent Times* (Grand Rapids: Eerdmans, 1995).

3. Richmond, VA: John Knox Press, 1967.

4. I employ *revivalism* here as Melton did, to refer to the American religious experience, especially that associated with late-nineteenth-century revivalism of

ship had previously been understood as a meeting between God and his visible people. Worship was a dialogue, if you will: God speaking through Word and sacrament, and his people responding in prayer, praise, and confession. The decisions that governed such worship revolved around this dialogical conception of worship as a meeting between God and his people.

According to Melton, revivalist meetings were quite different. While there might still be some elements in common with a worship meeting, a revivalist meeting was deliberately designed to attract the nonreligious, the unchurched, to a meeting where they would be challenged to consider embracing faith in Christ. These meetings were ordinarily held on a different day from Sunday, and were conceived as being essentially *different in kind* from the meeting of God and his people on the first day of the week.

After a generation, however, the two previous meetings became blended into one. Entire revivalist communions sprang up. Their meetings were largely revivalist meetings, though they still had some of the trappings of the earlier dialogue of worship. And other communions were influenced

---

the Dwight L. Moody sort, but recognizing roots in the earlier alleged awakenings associated with Jonathan Edwards and George Whitefield in the mid-eighteenth century, and in the later alleged awakenings of the late eighteenth and early nineteenth centuries, associated with such men as Charles Finney. While revivalism had roots in the seventeenth-century German Pietism of Philipp Jakob Spener and August Hermann Francke, it took on an even more anti-intellectual, individualistic, and anti-clerical form in its American expression. Cf. F. Ernest Stoeffler, *Continental Pietism and Early American Christianity* (Grand Rapids: Eerdmans, 1976); Dale W. Brown, *Understanding Pietism* (Grand Rapids: Eerdmans, 1978); Timothy L. Smith, *Revivalism and Social Reform: American Protestantism on the Eve of the Civil War* (Baltimore: Johns Hopkins University Press, 1980).

by revivalism, and began embracing some of its methods and emphases. This blended focus created some of the tension we experience in discussing music. If the purpose of a given hymn is to facilitate the dialogue between God and his people, the criteria by which we evaluate that hymn are different than if the purpose is to appeal to the unchurched. Indeed, no prayer (other than some version of a so-called sinner's prayer) would be appropriate for an unbeliever to pray. Could an unbeliever properly pray the prayer of general thanksgiving from the Anglican Book of Common Prayer, which reads in part: "We bless thee for our creation, preservation, and all the blessings of this life; but above all for thine inestimable love in the redemption of the world by our Lord Jesus Christ; for the means of grace, and for the hope of glory"? Can one without faith bless God for his inestimable love in redeeming us through Christ? Could an unbeliever conscientiously give thanks for either the means of grace or the hope of glory? The frequency of Communion is another question that gets caught in the cross fire of such a confused meeting. If, with Martin Luther, Thomas Cranmer, and John Calvin, we recognize that the apostolic church communed weekly (as the highest point and highest expression of a service that was itself a meeting and communion between God and his people), can the Lord's Supper function the same way in an evangelistic service?

Whatever evangelistic benefits we might hope to achieve by such a blended service (and I dispute them), we can probably agree that a meeting between God and his people becomes very different when those who are self-consciously not his people are invited not only to observe, but to participate and feel comfortable. As a meeting between God and his people, the meeting is compromised. As an analogy, suppose the members of a local Jewish synagogue determined to use their Saturday meetings to reach their neighborhood, so they designed a liturgy that avoided all the distinctives about Yahweh's relation to Israel: no mention of the exodus or Passover, nothing about the calling of Abram, the birth of Isaac, the tabernacle, temple, or Levites. This might make the visitor feel less an outsider, but it would severely compromise the synagogue as a meeting between Yahweh and the peculiar people he once called as his own.

Therefore, it might be wise to self-consciously rethink what kind of meeting is taking place on any given occasion, and to distinguish the meeting between God and his people from other meetings that have a consciously evangelistic purpose. This does not mean that unbelievers could not be invited to observe Christian worship; to the contrary, it might be very instructive and beneficial for them to witness a group of people in a meeting where those present believe that an invisible deity actually meets there with them and pledges his presence in a special way. There might even be a profound evangelistic effect from such observation. But there is an important difference between being invited as an *observer* and being invited as a *participant*. Some local synagogues, for instance, are gracious enough to permit people to attend their services as observers, to witness the Jewish tradition in its liturgical context. Such visitors are welcomed cordially, but they know they are not Jews, that this is not their tradition, not their religious "home." This is the way an unbeliever should feel in any service of religious worship: welcomed and loved, but still a "foreigner" or "stranger."

Seeker-Sensitive Services?

In the last few decades, a number of people have recommended what we now call *seeker-sensitive* services—services that are self-consciously designed to make an unbeliever (curiously, erroneously, and gratuitously referred to as a *seeker*) feel at home, to make religion seem less foreign. There is some merit to this approach. Unlike the unconscious blending of revivalist meetings with meetings between God and his people, at least this approach is self-aware that the two are distinct, and that the demands of the one and the demands of the other might differ. As a step toward self-consciousness, this is progress; and when such meetings are held *in addition to* (and not as a replacement of) the meeting of God and his people, there is no objection.

Even in such a circumstance, however, some clarifications are needed about the language employed. Does *seeker* equal *unbeliever*? Are all unbelievers seekers? Paul described our rebellious race this way: "No one seeks for God" (Rom. 3:11). This is important because it seems entirely appropriate to hold evangelistic meetings designed for *non*-seekers, people who at this point are *not* seeking religious faith or peace with God. That is, there are two categories of unbeliever, not one. There are those who have no particular interest in religion, and there are those who are genuinely at a point of aggressively seeking answers to the spiritual and religious issues of life. What the revivalist tradition calls *conversion* does not always (or even ordinarily?) happen in an instant; rather, there is a period or season of life in which some people become aware that something is missing, that the something may be peace with their Maker, and that they wish to see if there is a solu-

154

tion. How we would address the one is very different from how we would address the other; the way in which a cancer physician gives a talk on cancer awareness is different from how he addresses a patient who has cancer. So I might encourage the discussion of "non-seeker-friendly" meetings—meetings and activities with the short-term goal of creating true seekers, not addressing those who already are seekers.

The failure to make such a distinction creates an unintended irony: that those who are genuinely seeking for God are often repulsed by the so-called seeker-friendly services, which seem to be more about fun than about answering life's most serious question. Nothing is more serious than a person who is religiously seeking; such an individual is motivated by an existential intensity that makes all superficiality appear hyper-superficial. He is often deeply troubled by his condition, and is nearly desperate to know whether there is indeed an answer for his longings. For such an individual, a religious meeting that appears to treat religion as a trivial or insignificant thing is off-putting, not attractive.

I recall meeting with such an individual for a number of months when I was a pastor. A police officer, he and I played pool once or twice a month and sometimes had nice conversation over an ale afterward. On occasion, he attended my church. One evening after our playing pool, he told me that he was "not serious about religion," but that if he ever *became* serious about religion, he would attend my church. I asked him why, and he replied that he had attended some of the other churches in the area, and "they sit around in circles playing guitar and clapping, having fun, but they don't appear to take religion seriously. So if I ever *do* take religion seriously, I'll come to a place where they do also." He later did take religion seriously, attended our church for over a year before professing faith, and now, more than a decade later, is still a follower of Christ. Oddly enough, those very churches that thought they were being "seeker-friendly" were actually driving off individuals who were seekers.

Meeting People "Where They Are"

I frequently hear that there is some positive mandate, or at least an important strategic consideration, to meet people "where they are." I suppose this could be a shorthand way of repeating Martin Luther's concern that worship be conducted in a vernacular language, to ensure that people can follow it with intelligent understanding. If this were all it meant, I would surely endorse it. But I think it comes to mean another thing: that we not challenge anyone, anywhere, anytime to leave his or her comfort zone. We use no vocabulary beyond that of a typical grade-schooler, we preach no sermons beyond the average attention span of the typical American, and we surely make no moral demands (such as repentance) that might make an individual feel uncomfortable. Intellectually and aesthetically, that is, the church, by this reasoning, must not make anyone "stretch" or reach beyond his or her current attainments.[5]

It is not self-evident to me that this is or should be an unchallenged point of view. Some regard such a viewpoint as cynical and nonredemptive, as though such an approach were content to *leave* people "where they are." That is, if we "reach"

5. This is the concern expressed by Marva Dawn, *Reaching Out without Dumbing Down: A Theology of Worship for the Turn-of-the-Century Culture* (Grand Rapids: Eerdmans, 1995).

people where they are in our worship services, will there not be a regular influx of such people, so that we can never move beyond this to another level? The theory might say "reach them where they are," and then take them further, but will we ever in fact take them further? Will worship ever require and reward adult intelligence and sensibilities, if we feel obliged not to challenge people to develop them?

Is it not cynical to assume that people, at some level, do not *wish* to be challenged or stretched? Is not aspiration still part of ordinary human experience? At some level, do we not all wish to be wiser, more gracious, more just, more humble, and more intelligent? Is it not cynical to deny the existence of such aspiration? Consider the counterexample of Dr. John Broadus, one of the great ministers of the nineteenth century, a Southern Baptist associated with the founding of Southern Baptist Theological Seminary (originally in South Carolina; after the war it reopened in Louisville, Kentucky). He regularly refused to adopt such cynical practices, and deliberately chose to appeal to people's nobler aspirations. His vocabulary, reasoning, and other pulpit choices always aimed above the actual attainment of his hearers. When he died, one of the reviewers of his life noticed this trait in him:

> You feel yourself treated by the preacher with exquisite respect, not with flattery. It is the respect of a man who respects himself, as he also respects you, with nothing of the disagreeable effect of flattery. You insensibly respect yourself more, *not the self that you are, but the self that you ought to be*, and that you now begin to feel as if you might be. And it is that ideal man possible, rather than the far from ideal

man actual in you, that the preacher himself treats with such grave, such pathetic respect.[6]

Broadus treated his hearers with respect. He understood that their present attainments need not be regarded as their ultimate attainments, and he believed he could appeal to them as those who wished to improve, to grow, to broaden, to expand, not as those whose present attainments were their final attainments. Dr. Broadus's always aiming slightly "over their heads" was a means of prompting and facilitating their attainment of these nobler aspirations.

Reaching "the Young"

If I understand the matter correctly, part of the motivation behind the creation and use of contemporary worship music is concern not to "lose the youth."[7] The theory, I suppose, is that young people find traditional church music to be foreign-sounding and uninteresting; we can reach them only by employing pop-music forms. If we employ pop-music forms, they will attend church. Insofar as there is any truth in this theory, it resides in the reality that some young people will appreciate the gesture. They will notice that the church is making efforts to meet them on their own turf, so to speak, and they will rightly

6. Prof. W. C. Wilkinson, University of Chicago, in *Homiletic Review* (August–September 1888), emphasis mine.

7. Though even here, one must ask why no other generation manifested such a fear. As I indicated before, the church of my father's youth did not compose hymns in a big-band style in order to "reach the young," and the church of my generation, while quite aware of the 1960s rebellion against tradition, did not abandon its hymns to rewrite the hymnal to sound like Jimi Hendrix or Eric Clapton. So why do we constantly fear losing this particular generation if we do not employ musical idioms with which they are familiar?

appreciate such efforts. But many other precarious assumptions accompany this line of thought.

Practically speaking, in the first place, contemporary worship music is not the music of most young people, unless they are already churched and live in their own evangelical subculture in which they listen to Christian music exclusively. But other young people do not listen to music like contemporary worship music; hip-hop, rap, and the like are not musically analogous to contemporary worship music (despite the recurring efforts of Christian recording artists to emulate the latest trends, their music almost always sounds about a decade behind the curve). Young people who attend a church and see a group of fifty-year-olds playing their guitars in front of the church in order to "reach the young" will perhaps politely appreciate the gesture, but they frankly regard the music as being fairly lame.

In fact, many of them join me in perceiving not a well-considered approach to outreach, but a group of middle-aged former hippies who are simply unwilling to leave Woodstock in order to find Jesus. That is, the guitars are not for the young, but for the unwilling-to-be-no-longer-young. It is my generation who grooved to Pete Townshend's "My Generation," who had a profound sense of disconnect with our parents' generation, who insisted on rejecting their traditions and culture. Ours was the first generation to be musically weaned on the guitar, the first generation to reject any music not played on the guitar, the first to regard nonguitar music as unhip.

"Youth culture," that is, began with my generation. The notion of a separate youth culture is post-1950s. It is we, the middle-aged leadership of the church, who are blinded by our own experience, incapable of imagining that "the young" need not be segregated into their own culture but welcomed into the existing culture. We regard our own abnormality, our own adolescent resistance to joining adult culture and tradition, as a universal reality that we now impose on the next generation, without first consulting them to ask whether they wish to remain ghettoized in an adolescent world.

This ghettoizing of adolescence, which now extends for many into their early thirties, is due to many cultural factors, especially the various electronic-communications technologies and social-networking Web sites that have the effect of connecting adolescents to adolescents while disconnecting them from adults. This trend has been observed by thoughtful cultural analysts such as Maggie Jackson and Mark Bauerlein, the former of whom is concerned that it may lead to the next dark age, and the latter of whom suggests that it has produced "the dumbest generation."[8] The adults who created the plethora of electronic technologies and Web-based communication did not foresee that adolescents would use these media as an additional way to succumb to peer anxiety.

For my generation, peer anxiety was experienced only physically. If a group were gathered in the hallway, on the playground, or on the bus ride home, we did not wish to be excluded from it. But adolescents today are wired to one another "twenty-four seven," as they say. Adolescents today can be excluded (or *feel* that they are excluded, which is as bad) not only from physical gatherings, but also from electronic gatherings. They can be

8. Maggie Jackson and Bill McKibben. *Distracted: The Erosion of Attention and the Coming Dark Age* (New York: Prometheus Books, 2008); Mark Bauerlein, *The Dumbest Generation: How the Digital Age Stupefies Young Americans and Jeopardizes Our Future (Or, Don't Trust Anyone under Thirty)* (New York: Tarcher Press, 2008).

left out of IM, text messages, MySpace, Facebook, cell calls, YouTube videos, and so forth. They never really leave their adolescent friends or adolescent gossip to meet adults; they are imprisoned in an electronic society of adolescents, condemned and consigned to the social equivalent of *Lord of the Flies*. As Mark Bauerlein puts it:

> Instead of opening young American minds to the stores of civilization and science and politics, technology has contracted their horizon to themselves, to the social scene around them. Young people have never been so intensely mindful of and present to one another, so enabled in adolescent contact. Teen images and songs, hot gossip and games, and youth-to-youth communications no longer limited by time or space wrap them up in a generational cocoon reaching all the way into their bedrooms.[9]

Biblically, the goal of youth is to leave it as rapidly as possible. The goal of the young, biblically, is to be mature. "When I was a child, I spoke like a child, I thought like a child, I reasoned like a child. When I became a man, I gave up childish ways" (I Cor. 13:11). Biblical wisdom literature encourages the young to respect and emulate their seniors, not rebel against them. My generation tragically rejected such wisdom, and appears incapable of perceiving or repenting of its own unbiblical paedocentrism. We think, perhaps sincerely (though dull-wittedly), that we are "concerned for the youth," when we are actually concerned to preserve the cultural abnormality of youth *culture*. Because we naively preferred Hendrix to Haydn,

9. Bauerlein, *The Dumbest Generation*, 10.

Buffalo Springfield to Beethoven, we equally naively project the same error onto our children, and assume that they, too, will refuse to grow up and integrate themselves into the preexisting culture and tradition. We equate *youth* with *youth culture*, and erroneously believe that we cannot minister to the one without embracing, condoning, or promoting the other.

If we sincerely desire to "reach" young people, we should equally sincerely desire to reach them with a call to faith and repentance, by first repenting of our own paedocentrism. We should wish for better for our children than we experienced ourselves, and labor to relieve them of the burden of overextended adolescence. Our parents invited us to join them in a culture that had antedated both of our generations, and we politely (and sometimes impolitely) declined the invitation. But we are not even extending the invitation to our children's generation. To "reach" the young by propagating youth culture would be analogous to Jesus' "reaching" the rich young man by giving him money. Money was part of that particular sinner's problem, part of the reason he needed to be reached. Extended adolescence is part of what our youth need to be delivered *from*.

The element of truth expressed by those who propose contemporary-sounding music for strategic reasons is this: Many churches that employ traditional hymns do so very badly, and without apparent regard for this poor use of traditional hymns. Too often, for instance, someone will select a hymn because its lyrics seem to fit the theme of the sermon or some other aspect of the worship service, without regard for musical considerations such as these: Is the melodic range such that the average voice can sing it? (Anything over high E-flat is not singable.) Does the hymn have peculiar rhythms that make it hard for people to sing because they are counterintuitive? Can this melody be quickly learned, or must something be done to help? Will the accompanist play it at a singable tempo? If the accompanist plays too fast, or doesn't pause between verses, the congregation cannot breathe at appropriate places, and is therefore frustrated in the effort to sing. Similarly, if the accompanist plays too slowly, the congregation runs out of breath before completing some musical phrases, which is also frustrating.[10] If the congregation is not permitted to stand while singing, this will frustrate them because their diaphragms will not fully expand, and they will not be able to draw full breaths. Vocal soloists and choirs ordinarily stand while singing (as do players of wind instruments, if given the choice); the practice of sitting while attempting to sing will simply frustrate individuals. If people find the singing of traditional hymns frustrating, they will surely prefer to sing something else.

Further, is the particular traditional hymn good? The fact that it got into the hymnal does not guarantee that it is. Some hymns, regardless of their merit, have become popular, and a hymnal that omits them will not get used. So hymnal-revision committees ordinarily include some hymns that they themselves regard as "stinkers." Wise worship leaders will not include such hymns in the services of worship. They will select the best, most appropriate, most thoughtful and edifying of the available hymns (up to a fourth of the hymns in most hymnals would qualify). They will not select a poor hymn, or accompany it poorly, simply because "Mrs. Brown has always liked that one."

10. This issue of tempo is really not as difficult as it may appear, nor is a metronome the solution. The accompanist should play the hymns beforehand, singing along with them. If the accompanist becomes breathless, the tempo needs to be modified.

Such poor selectivity is part of what has driven some people to something else.

On far too many occasions, I have attended a church where an unfamiliar hymn was sprung on the congregation. Two or three measures into the hymn, the entire congregation stopped singing, and eventually the accompanist did also. This is dreadful and, in my judgment, inexcusable. If we wish to introduce hymns that are more difficult than the typical praise chorus, we must help people learn them. When I pastored, we did this fairly simply. Five or six weeks before introducing an unfamiliar hymn, I simply asked the pianist to play it as a prelude, postlude, offertory, or somewhere else each Sunday for the next month or so. Without even calling anyone else's attention to this, by the time we actually sang it, people had become familiar with the melody, the way people who have the radio on in the background begin to hum along with a pop-music song after they've heard it a few times.[11]

If the traditional hymns are pitched in an unsingable key, if the traditional hymns contain unusually difficult rhythms, if the tempo frustrates those attempting to sing it, if the introduction of new traditional hymns does not make some accommodation for the learning curve of the average congregant, many people will continue to gravitate to that which

11. At the bottom of our bulletins each Sunday, in small type, a single line read: "Next week's hymns:" followed by the numbers of those hymns. Thus, for any family or individual who desired to do so, there was opportunity to become more familiar beforehand. I still do not understand why every church doesn't do this simple thing. If even a small percentage of the congregation finds it helpful to meditate on the hymns beforehand, and if it takes no more work to select next week's hymns this week rather than next week, why not do it? Similarly, a choir might sing the first verse of a hymn, or sing the hymn during the collection a week or so before the congregation is introduced to it.

is more singable. As a strategic issue, then, defenders of traditional hymnody must expend substantially more effort than some do to ensure that the hymns they select are worthy of the congregation's effort, and that the hymns they select do not frustrate the congregation.

But the solution is not to abandon the rich heritage of the church's hymns for contemporary music. While contemporary music may sound familiar to many people, much contemporary worship music is not easier to sing. Often it is not accompanied by a written musical score, so a person who reads music cannot learn it except by listening to it. The singing of alto, bass, and tenor lines is ordinarily difficult in such music, which is not ordinarily composed with this in mind (most of it is essentially solo music that a group attempts to sing). Further, the guitar accompanist often riffs around between verses, so the congregation rarely attacks the introduction of each verse heartily. Much contemporary worship music is as difficult to sing, therefore, as many traditional hymns.

The most common argument for employing contemporary worship music is the strategic argument: to reach a culture captivated by pop music, the church must employ such music. But this argument, as we have just seen, is far from cogent. Most young people do not like this music nearly as much as adults think they do; many sincere seekers of religious truth find its playfulness and triviality off-putting; it is often more obstructive of congregational participation than its traditional counterpart; its casual character reflects and endorses a trivial culture rather than redemptively calling it to repentance and a narrow way. Since contemporary worship music has the many liabilities mentioned previously, its strategic benefits would have to be extraordinary in order to compensate for its liabilities. The meta-message liabilities of contemporary worship music, which tend to promote narcissism, paedocentrism, contemporaneity, and triviality, are significant barriers to overcome.

Strategically, at some point the church must reach people with the call to the narrow way of discipleship. It may wish to *reach* people "where they are," but it knows it cannot *leave* them where they are. "Where they are" is lost, analogous to where I was when my cancer surgeon told me that I had stage 3 cancer (with a 25 percent chance of survival).[12] Dr. Celebrezze was not interested in *reaching* me; he was interested in *saving* me, the first step of which was communicating the perilousness of my condition. If reaching people "where they are" appears to *endorse* "where they are," then it is the most significant strategic error the church can possibly make. At some point, it must mention taking up a cross daily, forsaking father and mother for Christ, and repentance. When the church approaches an individual as a consumer to be pleased, rather than as a recalcitrant sinner to be rescued, the church is no longer doing what it is called to do.

So perhaps there is an enormous strategic advantage to simply saying from the outset: "This is not a matter of consumption; it is not a matter of entertainment; it is not a matter of flattering your ego, your tastes, your habits, your lifestyle, or anything else. It is a matter of your finding peace with your Maker on his terms. The Christian gospel *offers* change, and indeed *demands* change; and the sooner you realize this, the better off you are. If you aren't ready to consider such change now,

12. For readers who do not know me, don't panic. I've recently had my five-year checkup and remain in cancer-free remission.

that's fine. When you *are* ready, come back and talk to us, and we will do our very best to help you then."

Questions for Reflection

1. Why did the author make the topic of strategic issues the final consideration, rather than the first consideration?

2. Why does the author object to such an apparently noble phrase as "reaching people for Christ"?

3. How and why did Julius Melton distinguish a worship meeting from a revival meeting? Can the two be easily combined? What is gained or lost in the process?

4. Can an unbeliever pray as a believer prays, or sing as a believer sings? Is it easy to compose prayers or hymns for a blended audience of believers and unbelievers? Explain.

5. Is there a valid distinction to be made between inviting an unbeliever to *observe* a service of worship and inviting such a person to *participate* in it? What is the effect of failing to make this distinction?

6. Are all unbelievers *seekers*? Are some unbelievers, at some moment, seekers? Would it be proper to have "non-seeker-friendly" services as part of the church's outreach? Why or why not? Are some seekers actually offended by seeker-friendly services? How?

7. If the church "reaches" people "where they are," is it ever easy for the church then to transition to taking them *beyond* "where they are"?

8. Are young people alone in demanding contemporary-sounding music, or does the hippie generation also demand

it? Which generation composed the song "My Generation"? How old is Pete Townshend, anyway?

9. Is "youth culture" a fairly old human phenomenon, or a fairly new one? Does anything in the teaching of Holy Scripture commend or promote such a culture?

10. What does it mean to ghettoize adolescents, and is it a good and helpful thing? Explain.

11. How does Maggie Jackson describe today's youth? How does Mark Bauerlein describe them?

12. Are all "traditional" hymns good? Are all easy for a congregation to sing?

13. Discuss: "The most common argument for employing contemporary worship music is the strategic argument: to reach a culture captivated by pop music, the church must employ such music. But this argument, as we have just seen, is far from cogent. Most young people do not like this music nearly as much as adults think they do; many sincere seekers of religious truth find its playfulness and triviality off-putting; it is often more obstructive of congregational participation than its traditional counterpart; its casual character reflects and endorses a trivial culture rather than redemptively calling it to repentance and a narrow way."

14. Discuss: "When the church approaches an individual as a consumer to be pleased, rather than as a recalcitrant sinner to be rescued, the church is no longer doing what it is called to do."

13

CONCLUDING THOUGHTS

NOT ONE OF THE CONSIDERATIONS I have raised, whether the form/content issues, contemporaneity issues, issues of triviality, or even more directly theological issues such as respect for earlier believers and their traditions, is a consideration so weighty as to suggest that contemporary worship music is sinful per se, or that it is unlawful to employ it under any circumstances. But the aggregate weight of these considerations is sufficient to give pause, and certainly their aggregate weight is sufficient to demonstrate that significant problems attend the rejection of traditional hymnody. In each of the specifics I mentioned earlier, much more could have been said. But I believe enough was said to indicate that whatever ostensible gains attend contemporary worship music, costs attend it also.[1]

1. And the greatest cost may be the implicit approval that such music gives to the un-Christian value of contemporaneity itself. If regarding earlier generations, traditions, or individuals with implicit contempt is un-Christian, then any artistic creation that contributes to such a value is also un-Christian. Westminster Larger Catechism 99 says, in part: "That under one sin or duty, all of the same kind are forbidden or commanded; together with all the causes, means, occasions, and appearances thereof, and *provocations thereunto*. That what is forbidden or commanded to ourselves, we are bound,

I am not alone in being concerned about the jettison-
ing of centuries of Christian hymnody, but I think I am
concerned for somewhat different reasons. Many others are
troubled about the fact that the matter has become somewhat divisive. I'm no fan of divisiveness, and I lament this
also. But other things bother me even more than this. I am
bothered that such a near-total change has taken place in
Christian worship in about two decades, without significant theological study. My grandfather, who died in 1979,
would not recognize the worship in perhaps the majority
of churches today. Should a change of such magnitude
happen so quickly? This has happened much faster than
the Protestant Reformation, for instance, yet where is the
intellectual and theological leadership of the quality of such
Renaissance-trained men as Martin Luther, John Calvin,
Jan Hus, and William Tyndale? How can a change of such
magnitude occur without several generations of serious
theological conversation?

I think I know the answer, and it comes from observers such
as Ken Myers, Todd Gitlin, and David Denby. The commercial
forces in our society have surrounded us with pop culture (as
a vehicle for their commercials), a culture that must resist that
which is beautiful and sublime (because it requires a learning curve), a culture that is merely trivial or inconsequential.
And our immersion in this culture, a culture that Gitlin says

---

according to our places, to *endeavor that it may be avoided or performed by others*, according
to the duty of their places" (emphases mine). If the common liturgical presence of
contemporary forms encourages us or others to embrace either aesthetic relativism or
contemporaneity, the presence of such qualities encourages those errors and, in the
language of the Assembly, is sinful.

"overwhelms" us,[2] has made Christians trivial also. We have unwittingly adopted the posture of pop culture that says that nothing is really serious. And if nothing is really serious, then worship is just something else that we consume—like Pepsi or Toyotas—and some people just like Pepsi more than Coke, or Toyota more than Chevrolet.

Yet if nothing is to be taken seriously, we have become impoverished, if not dehumanized. We've lost our capacity for the sublime, and have acclimated ourselves to the mundane, even to the point that we are not troubled when worship itself is mundane. We don't deny per se that worship has something to do with the sacred; we've lost the category of *the sacred* itself.

I'm also troubled that even educated people approach this issue with an almost willful refusal to entertain previous opinions of the church. Even educated people want to think that this is a "new question." Yet there's almost nothing new about it. The question of what constitutes a suitable or appropriate prayer or song for Christian worship is as old as the apostolic church. Paul addressed the Corinthians on the matter, for instance (I Cor. 14:14–17). Since the time of the apostles, the church has wrestled with how to create appropriate forms for use in Christian worship, whether those forms be prayers, salutations, confessions, creeds, absolutions, hymns, or benedictions. And as the church has discussed these matters, there has been substantial consensus, if not unanimity, on most of them. Regarding singing praise to God, every hymnal ever compiled has addressed the question of what constitutes an appropriate hymn; and some hymnals have even articulated their criteria in

2. Todd Gitlin, *Media Unlimited: How the Torrent of Images and Sounds Overwhelms Our Lives* (New York: Henry Holt and Company, 2002).

the opening pages. So the conversation about what standards we erect to evaluate potential church music is simply not new; it is old. Yet why do we not care what others in the history of the church have said? Why do we erect one criterion only—that a hymn sound contemporary (ordinarily, by accompanying it with a guitar)—and in the process exclude all the other criteria that have been proposed and adopted by the church for centuries? And further, why do we (unlike the Reformers) do so without demonstrating that the previous churches were *errant* in the criteria they proposed?

There is, of course, no reasonable answer to this line of questions; there is only cultural explanation. Ours is a contemporaneous culture—hook, line, and sinker. Nearly all the mediating institutions of our culture regard the past with contempt: the past is passé.[3] We don't disagree with the past; we just pay no attention to it. It was primitive, it was pre-electronic, and it "wouldn't understand us today." Well, these primitive, pre-electronic people were still humans, still made in God's image, and still poised precariously between his judgment and grace, just as we are, and it is little more than self-congratulatory folly and hubris to assume that we can learn nothing from them. It is especially hubristic to do so at our present moment in history.

The twentieth century was the greatest killing century of all time. A larger percentage of the population of the planet was put to death by others than ever before—and this was just

3. Even a supposedly conservative institution such as the one I serve recently altered its language requirement to disallow Latin and Greek, languages (I suppose) hopelessly shrouded in cobwebs. What could we possibly learn from ancient Greeks or Romans?

the genocides, without adding the wars.[4] So why would we, of all generations that ever lived, be so confident that we've got it figured out, whatever "it" is? We may be less primitive than previous generations, but we are manifestly more murderously barbaric than they.

If our wisest theologians and best musicians had studied the criteria adopted by the various hymnal committees of the church's past, and if this blue-ribbon group returned with a judgment that one or another of the previous criteria was wrong for some reason, I would be more than willing to hear their report. But this has not been done. We have rejected their criteria without first even asking what they were. Johnny hasn't been persuaded that hymn-singing is *wrong*; Johnny simply cannot *relate* to anything that doesn't sound contemporary. He cannot shed his cultural skin, the skin of contemporaneity, of triviality, of paedocentrism. He thinks he "prefers" contemporary worship music to other forms, but in reality he prefers contemporaneity as a trout prefers water; it is the only environment he knows. In roughly twenty-five years, Christian worship has gone from being serious to being casual—not because a case has been cogently or theologically argued that "casual" is more appropriate to a meeting with God, but because the culture itself has become casual, and the church has chosen not to resist the cultural inertia. David Letterman doesn't take anything seriously—why should we?

It is not merely the case that Johnny *doesn't* sing hymns. It is truer to say that Johnny *cannot* sing hymns. Johnny has been so swallowed up in a contemporaneous, casual, trivial,

4. Lewis M. Simons, "Genocide and the Science of Proof," *National Geographic*, 209, No. I (January 2006): 28.

youth-centered, guitar-playing pop culture that for him, *music*, by definition, sounds contemporary. Cut off in any meaningful way from music that does not sound contemporaneous outside church gatherings, Johnny is simply incapable of making the leap within those gatherings to musical genres with which he is otherwise entirely unacquainted. Johnny is monogenerational outside the church; so he is monogenerational inside the church. Outside the church, he lives in heedless disregard for those who have preceded him; why should it be any different inside the church? Perhaps Johnny suffers from contemporary insanity. Perhaps he is ill in some ways. If so, a redemptive institution such as the church should minister to him and heal him, binding his psychological wounds and restoring him to cultural, social, and psychological health.

Perhaps not surprisingly, since Johnny is inundated by electronic technologies and messages that immerse him in the present, he has little regard for the past. The changes of his generation, or so he thinks, are so great as to render the past passé. But let's just test that theory. Suppose we allow our imaginations to wander across the pages of history for a moment, asking this question: What generation, in the entire history of the human race, would have been justified in regarding itself as so new and distinctive that the past could be discarded? What generation, in other words, would have witnessed such new realities that everything prior to it could be dismissed as passé? Surely it would be the apostolic generation. God had come to earth in Jesus of Nazareth, lived and supped with us, died unjustly and cruelly. Most importantly, the Crucified One rose from the grave three days later. Truly, this changed everything.

And yet, were those of the apostolic generation contemporaneous? Though their day truly witnessed "new creation," though truly at that moment the old had passed away and "behold, the new ha[d] come" (2 Cor. 5:17), they were not contemporaneists at all. Almost every page of the New Testament makes reference to the Old Testament, and the forty verses of Hebrews 11 do not place before our consideration a single New Testament saint, but instead urge our consideration of Abel, Enoch, Noah, Abraham and Sarah, Isaac, Jacob, Esau, Joseph, Moses, Gideon, Barak, Samson, Jephthah, David, Samuel, the prophets, and others "of whom the world was not worthy" (v. 38). Though contemporary with the most significant event in human history, the members of the apostolic generation did not disregard the individuals or traditions that antedated them. As soon as Johnny persuades me that cell phones, laptop computers, or PDAs are more significant than Christ's empty tomb, I will join him in his contemporary insanity. Until then, we should offer him asylum in the church, hoping and trusting that there his poor, rootless soul will discover the sanity of communing with an everlasting God and the saints of all ages.

If we return, imaginatively, to my father's Depression-era generation, the point would be this: those of my father's generation, by the sheer accidents of their circumstances, heard a variety of musical forms, none of which especially predominated. If anything, the most common music heard by that generation was sacred music; at least weekly, they sang hymns in church. We live in a profoundly different culture—a culture where many of our daily activities (shopping, working, amusement/ entertainment) are accompanied by pop music. By far, pop music is the prevailing, almost exclusive idiom of music in our culture. It is, ordinarily, all that Johnny hears. Johnny's culture, compared to my father's, is impoverished both by its musical sameness and by the reality that the prevailing form of music is fairly trivial.[5] The church's challenge, in such a setting, is to decide whether it wishes to be complicit in this impoverishment of the human experience, or whether it is willing to be a voice crying in the wilderness, at least once weekly providing an alternative to an impoverished culture.

It should be evident which of the decisions I believe the church should make. At a minimum, however, these thoughts have been designed to remove the conceit, so frequently and erroneously repeated, that this is "just a matter of taste." This issue is not a matter of taste; it is a matter of serious aesthetic, theological, and liturgical principle. To choose contemporary worship music over traditional worship music is to *reject* the criteria proposed by all those generations of hymn-writers and hymn-compilers. Such a wholesale rejection, without a season of theological (and musical) reflection analogous to that which informed the Reformation, has been a disservice both to the church and to the world.

Questions for Reflection

1. Was the recent movement to contemporary worship music the result of years of theological reflection? Was it the result of a compelling Reformer, such as Martin Luther or John Calvin? Was it the result of denominational study

5. That is, if we heard only one idiom of music, and that idiom was classical, for instance, we would be comparatively less impoverished. Being restricted to merely one idiom is not to be desired, but some idioms are themselves richer than others, musically speaking.

committees? Where does the author locate the source of the transformation?

2. Discuss and debate the author's claim: "The conversation about what standards we erect to evaluate potential church music is simply not new; it is old. Yet why do we not care what others in the history of the church have said?"

3. On what basis does the author dispute the conceit that the twentieth century was the greatest and most humane century of all time?

4. Discuss and debate the author's claim: "Johnny simply cannot *relate* to anything that doesn't sound contemporary. He cannot shed his cultural skin, the skin of contemporaneity, of triviality, of paedocentrism."

5. According to the author, which generation, in all of human history, might have been justified in being contemporaneous? Was that generation in fact contemporaneous? How do you know?

6. Discuss and debate the author's primary thesis: "This issue is not a matter of taste; it is a matter of serious aesthetic, theological, and liturgical principle. To choose contemporary worship music over traditional worship music is to *reject* the criteria proposed by all those generations of hymn-writers and hymn-compilers."

14

TEACHING JOHNNY HYMNODY

THIS IS NOT INTENDED as a practical book, in the "how-to" sense. It is designed to describe how we got where we are now, and to make a case that, regarding worship music, where we are now is not so good. I recognize, however, that some of my readers may be like some of my students. They will be persuaded that my lament is justified, and they will say, as many of my students have: What do we do now? Here are a few thoughts on that question.

First, we must take what is implicit and make it explicit. Much of this book consists of describing a variety of cultural forces and implied values of which many people, lay or clergy, are unaware. Many of us may have never really thought of pop music, for instance, as a particular musical idiom. We have probably recognized that classical music is an idiom, and probably noticed that jazz is a different idiom, but we may not recognize that pop is its own idiom. Similarly, many of us are unaware of the relationship between commerce and pop culture, and we may be unaware of contemporaneity as a profound cultural value and force. And few of us, unless we are sociologists or media ecologists, are aware of the form-content or "meta-message" issues raised here.

Therefore, those who become persuaded that the church's worship would be enriched either by abandoning contemporary music altogether or by diminishing its ratio in the mixture of forms will need to begin to discuss explicitly what otherwise remains hidden to most members of our churches. We must especially be willing to both develop and teach a biblical perspective on singing praise. At a minimum, we must persuade our parishioners that singing God's praise is a solemn duty. It is something we do because God commands it. Therefore, the controlling criterion must be the same in any such matter: what would please God more? Because music is so closely associated with entertainment in our culture, it is entirely understandable that for many people, music is just another consumer choice, and each individual is free to make such a choice. But worship music is not entertainment, it is not consumption, it is not passive. Until such implied (but unexpressed and unargued) values are put "on the table," I think little progress can be made.

Second, we must exercise the pastoral patience of John Calvin during the Reformation. In his letters, Calvin often expressed frustration over the fact that the Reformation had made so little progress in reforming the churches by a biblical standard. In each case, however, he also indicated that if the Reformation proceeded at too fast a pace, the people would be left behind, because people cannot change too much too quickly. If, in a church accustomed to exclusively contemporary music in worship, we suddenly on a given Sunday replaced all of it with traditional hymns, we would likely accomplish little more than emptying the building. Perhaps in such settings it is best to simply introduce one well-selected traditional hymn a week, a hymn that has enjoyed the widespread consensus of much of the Christian tradition. A brief sentence or two in the bulletin about its composer or the circumstances of its composition, indicating how or why the church has found it edifying, might be helpful also.

That is, the mere introduction of the church's historic hymnody to the service of worship, without training, education, or explanation, will simply not do. In every other area of our Christian faith and life, we are patient with one another, and pastors are patient with their flocks. We introduce change slowly and purposefully, and we thoroughly and candidly discuss the reasons for doing so before we make the change. When I took my pastorate in New Hampshire, for instance, I indicated to the officers two changes I might wish to see take place in that congregation's worship (one of which was to introduce frequent Communion); and all I asked was permission to make the argument to the officers after three years, and then ask them to make a decision after another two years. They ended up asking for my reasoning much earlier, became persuaded, and then asked me to instruct the church for a number of months about worship in general, and these changes specifically. The changes were implemented without any disruption in our fellowship, and without losing a single individual.

All Christian change, whether individual or congregational, proceeds on the assumption that God will be pleased with progress, even if the progress is somewhat slow. The best outcome occurs when, as a result of patient instruction, the people become persuaded and virtually request the change. The next best occurs when not all of them become persuaded that the change is necessary, but at least become persuaded that it is both lawful and very well considered. People can often tolerate a change that is manifestly well considered and thoughtful, even when they are not yet entirely persuaded that it is right.

Third, we must seek the assistance of musicians in making wise choices regarding hymnody. Note that I say *musicians*, in the plural, because there are sometimes honest differences of opinion among musicians, and differing areas of expertise. There might even be some nonperforming musicians who understand musical properties well enough to have important counsel to give.

As an example, if one listens to pop music, ordinarily sung by an individual lead singer, one often hears the singer "slide" into a pitch, by beginning slightly off the pitch, and gradually modulating the voice into the pitch. Frank Sinatra was not only famous for this, but also infamous for frequently failing to find the proper pitch at the end! While I think this stylistic device is overused (it has become a virtual musical cliché), it is far less objectionable with a solo voice than with a chorus. The soloist is free to slide at will, using his or her own musical judgment as to when to resolve the pitch; but a group of singers can almost never time this move precisely, and the entire thing becomes messy.

As another example, note what happens when a traditional hymn is accompanied by a guitar. The rhythmic strumming of a guitar, and the chords so strummed, sometimes renders it confusing, if not impossible, for the singers to sing anything but the melody. If the oblique parts are polyphonic, the rhythms of those parts often conflict with the rhythms of the guitar-strumming, which would not happen if the hymn were accompanied, for instance, on a piano. Similarly, the chords selected by the guitarist may conflict with the harmonies in those oblique parts. Thus, the musical choice to accompany with a guitar has the effect of discouraging the singing of parts—a discouragement that should not occur apart from some deliberate choice.[1]

Very closely related to this is the widespread tendency in churches today to publish only the lyrics (not the musical score) in a bulletin or on an overhead projection of some sort. The effect is to greatly reduce both congregational participation and harmony.[2] If the musical score is not published, those who are unfamiliar with the hymn cannot sing it until they've heard it a few times, whereas if the musical score is printed, those of us who read music have little difficulty in singing robustly a piece of music never heard before. If the

1. I candidly recognize that cogent arguments have been made for unison-only singing. In ecclesiastical circles where that argument has been consciously embraced, I have no objection to unison-only singing. But since I do not, myself, embrace the argument, I consider it objectionable for the *practice* of a church to be unison-only when the *theory* of the same church is not unison-only.

2. Such a practice also often vitiates the biblical concern for intelligent singing because sometimes less than an entire sentence or verse appears at a time. How can one intelligently sing a sentence without knowing how the sentence ends? Suppose, as an illustration, the first verse of a hymn praises the Father, the second the Son, the third the Spirit, and the fourth the Trinity as a whole. If singing from a printed hymnal, the singer can quickly notice the carefully Trinitarian composition of the hymn and can intelligently sing each verse, aware of the concluding Trinitarian stanza. But this cannot be done if the lyrics are flashed up several words or phrases at a time.

musical score is not printed, it is nearly impossible for the tenor, bass, and alto parts to be sung, since those parts are not always self-evident.

As a third example, the key and range in which congregational music is written is a very significant matter. On occasion, a guitarist will choose a key that has either easier fingering for the chords or a more comfortable range for his or her own voice. But that comfort level may be entirely unsuited to the average voice of the average singer in the average congregation. One hesitates to give Mosaic proscriptions here, but a fair rule of thumb is this: "Thou shalt not require the congregation to sing above an E-flat." If a hymn melody goes up to an E-natural or F, many people today simply cannot reach it, and they switch to an octave down, and keep switching back and forth (like an automatic transmission without enough transmission fluid), because the entire song cannot be sung an octave lower, and parts of it cannot be sung in the octave the accompanist has chosen. When I pastored, and encountered such hymns on occasion, I simply transposed the hymn into another key for the accompanist, who played it a step or two lower than what was written in the hymnal. This would hopefully have bothered only those with perfect pitch (and admittedly, it would have driven them utterly crazy). More preferable is simply to find an edition of the hymn that is written in a singable key in the first place.

A musician, then, understands which musical *properties* or options are conducive to congregational and choral music and which are not. A musician knows which musical scores are more accessible to (can be sung by) a congregation than others. A musician can step back and raise the question whether a proposed hymn, chorus, or song creates barriers to congregational singing.

Many churches that employ traditional hymns, in my estimation, would benefit greatly from some musical counsel. Sometimes these hymns are written in unsingable keys; occasionally they reflect rhythmic properties that are extremely unfamiliar today; and occasionally they have melodic intervals that are unexpected, and therefore difficult for a congregation to sing. Introducing hymns to a congregation without the oversight of a skilled musician will most often lead to a frustrating experience for the congregation.

If a congregation can be persuaded that contemporaneity itself is a sub-Christian and impoverishing value, if a congregation can be persuaded that the providence of God affords us a rich tradition of extremely edifying Christian hymnody, if a few musicians will occasionally answer a few questions, and if a pastoral staff is patient in instruction and implementing gradual change, I see nothing to prevent a renewal or renaissance in the appreciation of traditional hymnody in the churches. Johnny can learn to sing hymns, and learn to be richly blessed by them. Johnny may have been temporarily befuddled by a commercial, paedocentric, contemporaneous, pop culture— but biblical light can bring him understanding and clarity in the matter of hymnody, as that light has illuminated in many other matters before.

Questions for Reflection

1. Why does the author, though no proponent of contemporary worship music, say: "The mere introduction of

the church's historic hymnody to the service of worship, without training, education, or explanation, will simply not do"?

2. What was John Calvin's approach to the reformation of the church's worship?

3. Discuss the likely consequences of each method of change: (1) patiently, and with much instruction; and (2) imposed as an exercise of ecclesiastical authority.

4. In many churches, the musicians are primarily performers. What role does the author recommend for them?

APPENDIX

THE FOLLOWING TABLE is taken from Kenneth A. Myers, *All God's Children and Blue Suede Shoes: Christians and Popular Culture* (Westchester, IL: Crossway Books, 1989), 120.

As helpful as this table is, as a summary of many of the realities discussed in the book itself, it is no substitute for reading the book. The table inevitably summarizes and generalizes what Myers, in the text itself, treats with great nuance and sophistication. Those intrigued by the following table will surely wish to read the book itself in its entirety.

Kenneth A. Myers on Pop versus Classical Culture

POPULAR CULTURE	TRADITIONAL AND HIGH CULTURE
Focuses on the new	Focuses on the timeless
Discourages reflection	Encourages reflection
Pursued casually to "kill time"	Pursued with deliberation
Gives us what we want, tells us what we already know	Offers us what we could not have imagined
Relies on instant accessibility; encourages impatience	Requires training; encourages patience
Emphasizes information and trivia	Emphasizes knowledge and wisdom
Celebrates fame	Celebrates ability
Appeals to sentimentality	Appeals to appropriate, proportioned emotions
Content and form governed by the requirements of the market	Content and form governed by the requirements of the created order
Formulas are the substance	Formulas are the tools
Relies on spectacle, tending to violence and prurience	Relies on formal dynamics and the power of symbols (including language)
Aesthetic power in reminding of something else	Aesthetic power in intrinsic attributes
Individualistic	Communal
Leaves us where it found us	Transforms sensibilities
Incapable of deep or sustained attention	Capable of repeated, careful attention
Lacks ambiguity	Allusive, suggests the transcendent
No discontinuity between life and art	Relies on "Secondary World" conventions
Reflects the desires of the self	Encourages understanding of others
Tends toward relativism	Tends toward submission to standards
Used	Received

T. David Gordon (MAR, ThM, Westminster Theological Seminary; PhD, Union Theological Seminary in Virginia) is professor of religion and Greek at Grove City College, where since 1999 he has taught courses in religion, Greek, humanities, and media ecology. Prior to that, he taught New Testament (primarily Pauline studies) for thirteen years at Gordon-Conwell Theological Seminary, and for nine years he was pastor of Christ Presbyterian Church in Nashua, New Hampshire.

Dr. Gordon has contributed to a number of books and study Bibles (his notes on John's gospel appear in the *New Geneva Study Bible* and the *Reformation Study Bible*) and has published scholarly reviews and articles in journals such as *New Testament Studies, The Westminster Theological Journal, Interpretation,* and *Journal for the Evangelical Theological Society.* His popular articles have appeared in periodicals such as *Modern Reformation, Tabletalk, Decision,* and *Lay Leadership.*

With his wife Dianne he attends Grace Anglican Church in Slippery Rock, Pennsylvania.